D1617465

# A Survival Guide to the Prado Museum

By Jeffery Barrera

Dedicated to my mother, who taught me to love museums.

## Table of Contents

## Introduction

In this guidebook you will find a selection of commented paintings. The selection is personal and it is backed by my robust education in art and art history. This is a selection of paintings that I appreciate, enjoy or just plain love in the museum. These are the paintings that I would like to share with you.

The selection includes most of the museum's masterpieces and better-known paintings. However, you will also find several paintings, which don't usually make the cut for Prado guidebooks. I would like to add that this was not an easy task, selecting the 20 paintings and 14 artists that I have included in this guide, considering that there are over 7.000 paintings in the Prado's collection.

Most likely you will not fully agree with my selection. Indeed, you may even believe I have missed out on several important ones (paintings or artists) that should have been included. Indeed, how can I justify leaving out Raphael or Tintoretto? If this is the case, than I will have happily achieved one of the aims of this guide: that of wetting your appetite for more – perhaps triggering a pleasant debate about the Prado's collection.

This is not a comprehensive guide for the Prado but a guide meant to enhance your visit, which is usually limited to a couple of hours, and the aim of this book is that you leave the museum feeling you have not wasted your time and that perhaps you even had a good time.

## A Survival Guide: Why?

One of the most common clichés when talking to someone about art is that they state that they don't like art or enjoy museums because they *don't understand it*. This statement is sometimes followed by a subtle self-reproach admitting that they wish they did; although the statement is also frequently followed by a blunt *art is boring* that usually terminates the conversation.

And yet, every time I go to the Prado (or any other major European museum), there are almost always crowds of people wandering around inside or patiently queuing outside (frequently in the rain and cold!). The same people that say that they don't understand art and don't enjoy museums are willing to forfeit a whole morning or afternoon of their vacation time in the museum. The reasons for this are baffling (to me at least).

Even more baffling are the museum guidebooks. I have found that museum guidebooks tend to work as deterrents from enjoying art and the museum. Museum guidebooks usually take too much for granted, requiring prior knowledge of art and art history from the reader/visitor; or just get lost in facts and information that are of no interest to a person on vacation. They are also usually written in a dull academic literary style, detached from the visitor and unconcerned about empathising with the visitor. Or in other words, museum guidebooks tend to be plain boring.

Here's an example:

The current online Prado gallery describes *Las Meninas* (arguably the Prado's signature masterpiece) as,

*"... a complex composition built with admirable skill in the use of perspective, the depiction of light, and the representation of atmosphere."*

Most likely, if you have not studied Velázquez and his *Meninas*, this makes very little sense to you. And what does *representation of atmosphere* mean?

Another example can be found in the current official Prado guidebook that finds it necessary to name all the people in the *The Meninas*. Do we really care what the nun's name was? I don't (and for the record, her name was Marcela de Ulloa). Or do we really care that the paintings in the background on the wall are copies of copies of paintings by Rubens and Jordaens?

*A Survival guide to the Prado Museum* is a guide for the untrained, for those that believe they don't understand art, and for those that have ended up having to (or wanting to) spend some time in the Prado, and who also want to make the most of their visit.

This does not mean that this guide is not rigorous. On the contrary, everything you read here has been verified and is supported by expert opinions. Likewise, you may not agree with everything you read, indeed, you may even find some of the information surprising. That's perfectly OK, there is no universal truth in art and most paintings are open to a diversity of interpretations (even if the experts don't agree with you).

In summary, with this guide I don't aim to instruct you in art, but hopefully spark enough interest in what you are looking at so as to make your visit more enjoyable.

And remember that you are visiting the greatest art museum in the world, and that is my shamefully biased opinion!

## The greatest art museum in the world

My prior statement that the Prado is the greatest museum in the world is based on the following facts:

1. Contrary to other great art museums around the world, the bulk of the Prado collection is made up by the Spanish royalty's private collection (first the Habsburg dynasty and later the Bourbon), this provides the collection with a rare sense of cohesion.

2. The Spanish Habsburg's were not only the most powerful and wealthy dynasty in Europe when they reigned but were also avid art collectors; meaning that they had the means to purchase and commission from the best.

3. The Habsburgs also ruled over regions in Europe that were not Spanish, such as the Netherlands and parts of Italy. This facilitated the Spanish Court's access to Flemish and Italian art, arguably the two most important art schools in Europe (along with the Spanish one) between the 15th and 17th centuries.

4. After the Italian Renaissance (15th and 16th century), the greatest moment in classic art history may have been the Spanish Baroque (17th century), and all of it is here (well, almost all of it).

5. Other museums have *lots* of paintings and *some* masterpieces. The Prado is smaller in size, has less paintings but proportionally it has more masterpieces than any other museum (the Uffizi in Florence is a very near second place).

6. The size of the Prado makes it much more manageable and less overwhelming than other museums, such as the Louvre.

7. Almost all of Goya and Velázquez are here, and that is reason enough to spend a couple hours inside.

# Art Timeline from the Middle Ages to the 20th Century

The following is a basic outline of the different art periods in Europe from the Middle Ages to the 20th century.

11th to 13th century - **Romanesque**

13th to 14th century - **Gothic**

15th century - **Early Renaissance**

16th century - **Renaissance**

17th century – **Baroque** and **Mannerism**

18th century - **Neoclassicism**

19th century – **Romanticism**, **Realism** and **Impressionism**

20th century – **Avant-garde art**

# How to use this guide

Each painting corresponds to a chapter. There are 20 commented paintings, which correspond to 20 chapters. Each chapter is headed by the painter's name followed by the title of the painting and an image of the painting being commented. Please note that as you should have the painting in front of you, the image I have included should only serve identification purposes (hence the low image resolution). All of this is followed by a commentary of the painting.

**Each commentary is just over a 1000 words long, although, if you feel you are short of time, I suggest you limit your reading time in the museum to the first three headings that are common for each painting: a)** *What's the picture about?*, **b)** *Elements in the painting*, **and c)** *Why have I included this painting in this guide?*

The chapters **are ordered following two suggested routes described** below. However, you can easily alter this route and navigate to each chapter in any sequence by returning to the Table of Contents. Just tap on the link at the end of the chapter.

**A map for each route is described in the next chapter:** *Navigating the Prado*

I have suggested a shorter route (**Route A**) that covers **10 paintings** and should take you around an hour and half to complete. These are the paintings included on **Route A** and they are listed in the order you will see them:

1. *Adam and Eve* by Durer
2. *The Triumph of Death* by Bruegel
3. *The Garden of Earthly Delights* by Bosch
4. *Philip II* by Sofonisba Anguissola
5. *Hare Hunt* by Anonymous (Romanesque painting)
6. *The Dog* by Goya
7. *Fable* by El Greco
8. *Venus and the Organist* by Titian
9. *The Meninas* by Velázquez
10. *The Three Graces* by Rubens

If you have more time, there are **another 10 paintings** on **Route B**. It should take you up to 3 hours to appreciate all 20 paintings included in this guide (**Route A + Route B**)

These are the other 10 paintings listed in order that you would add to the previous list:

11. *The Story of Nastagio Degli Onesti, Part 1* by Botticelli
12. *The Descent from the Cross* by Van der Weyden
13. *The Last Supper* by Juan de Juanes
14. *3rd of May 1808* by Goya
15. *Vulcan's Forge* by Velázquez
16. *Crucifixion* by Velázquez
17. *Nude Maja* by Goya
18. *Sisyphus* by Titian
19. *Democritus* by Ribera
20. *The Birth of St. John the Baptist* by Gentileschi

A final suggestion on the correct use of this guide: take your time and stop at paintings that are not in the guide. Your favourite paintings may not be in my selection.

## Navigating the Prado

The Prado is easy to navigate (it really is). Its floor plan is basically one large hall with rooms adjacent on one side of the hall and a few rooms at both ends. The building has two stories (well, three, but you can ignore the third one) and the top floor has roughly the same layout as the bottom floor. So if you get your bearings on the ground floor, just do the same thing upstairs.

I have included below a museum map of the museum with the location of the commented paintings. However, the museum moves paintings around when it feels like it, or loans paintings for exhibits or rotates paintings in and out of storage. So if the painting is not where I say it is, it may be in another room, on loan or stored away.

The Prado offers **free Museum Maps** and a helpful information desk that should have up to date information of where everything is.

**My suggestion is that once you have gone through security, step over to the Information desk just across the hall and pick up a free Museum Map in English. Using my museum maps (below) and the official Museum Map, you should not have any problems navigating the museum and finding the paintings.**

If you entered the museum from the bottom floor (which I recommend), you will always enter the exhibit halls through a brightly painted red room. You should start your visit going straight through that room and turning right into the Main Hall (room 49 on your Museum Map).

If you entered the museum from the top floor, then start your visit with the paintings on the top floor and make your way down. As you enter the museum on the top floor, you will see the Main Hall in front of you (Rooms 24 to 29 on the Museum Map).

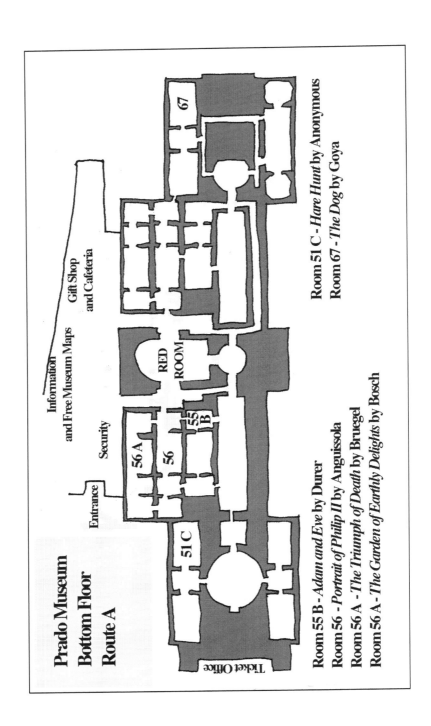

Prado Museum
Bottom Floor
Route A

Entrance

Security

Information
and Free Museum Maps

Gift Shop
and Cafeteria

51 C

56 A

56

55 B

RED ROOM

67

Ticket Office

Room 55 B - *Adam and Eve* by Durer
Room 56 - *Portrait of Philip II* by Anguissola
Room 56 A - *The Triumph of Death* by Bruegel
Room 56 A - *The Garden of Earthly Delights* by Bosch

Room 51 C - *Hare Hunt* by Anonymous
Room 67 - *The Dog* by Goya

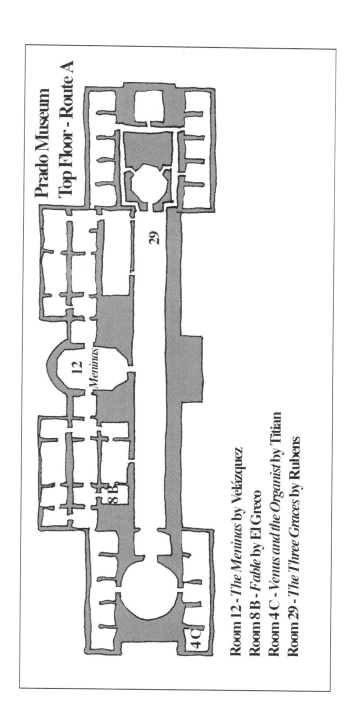

**Prado Museum**
**Top Floor - Route A**

Room 12 - *The Meninas* by Velázquez
Room 8 B - *Fable* by El Greco
Room 4 C - *Venus and the Organist* by Titian
Room 29 - *The Three Graces* by Rubens

19

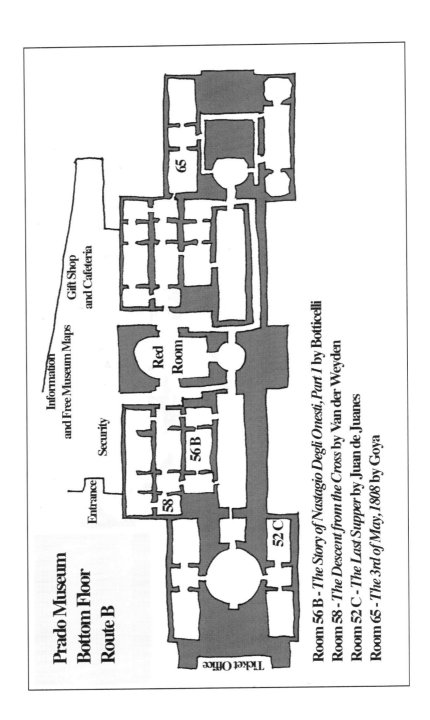

Prado Museum
Bottom Floor
Route B

Room 56 B - The Story of Nastagio Degli Onesti, Part 1 by Botticelli
Room 58 - The Descent from the Cross by Van der Weyden
Room 52 C - The Last Supper by Juan de Juanes
Room 65 - The 3rd of May, 1808 by Goya

20

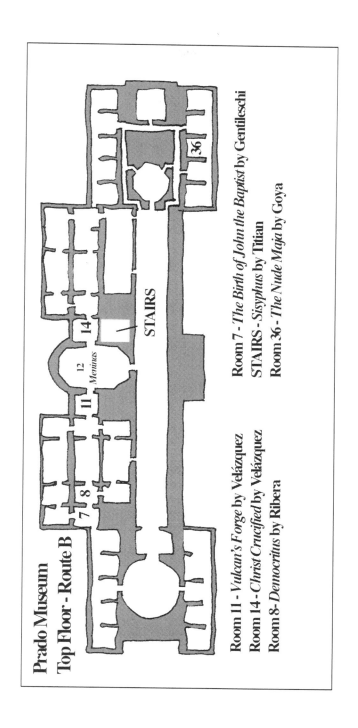

**Prado Museum**
**Top Floor - Route B**

Room 11 - *Vulcan's Forge by Velázquez*
Room 14 - *Christ Crucified by Velázquez*
Room 8 - *Democritus by Ribera*

Room 7 - *The Birth of John the Baptist by Gentileschi*
STAIRS - *Sisyphus by Titian*
Room 36 - *The Nude Maja by Goya*

## 1. Adam and Eve by Durer

Bottom floor - Room 55 B – Route A

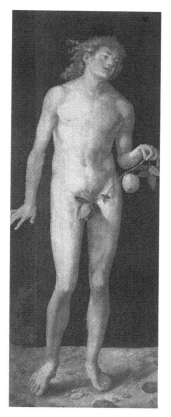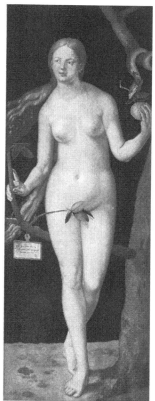

## What's the picture about?

This painting is a representation of the ideal woman and man (anatomically perfect and physically pleasing to the eye) in 16th century Germany. It also depicts the moment that Adam is about to eat from the apple, which Eve has given him, thus provoking their ejection from the Garden of Eden (according to the book of Genesis in the Bible).

Late medieval religious paintings in Europe tended to shun female nudity, only tolerating it where necessary for narrative accuracy, such as the story of Adam and Eve. When women were depicted nude, the figures usually fell into either the category of women that were descriptively painted (almost sticklike figures without clothes on with their female attributes highlighted such as long hair or breasts) or women that were depicted anatomically correct but ignoring essential physical female differences (such as wider hips or a less defined muscle tone). All of this changed slowly in the early Renaissance as artists discovered that they would not be stoned or tortured by Church authorities for painting nude women who looked like women (in theory at least).

But the problem still remained in finding nude female models. Any art student knows that it is impossible to correctly imagine a nude body for a drawing or a painting and as you can imagine, there were not a whole lot of women that were allowed to pose nude in artist's studios. In fact, women were not allowed to pose nude in academic workshops till the 18th century. So until then artists made use of male models (preferably younger ones) and then imagined the rest. Or, as it is clear in the case of Durer's *Eve*, found some way around this conundrum.

Likewise, Durer's *Eve* is not your standard archetypical Eve. Durer has reinterpreted the story and presents us with an enticing young female with her hair blowing in the wind (who looks like an enticing young female even for our current standards) in an almost playful mood (note the hint of a smile and the little step or dance she is doing as she takes the apple without even glancing at the snake). Durer has painted a story of seduction between Adam and Eve (note Adam's stupefied stare as he looks at Eve, even after having taken the apple) and not the story of the greatest tragedy of Christian history: the downfall of man (and woman). Or in other words, Durer has used a Biblical story with nudes to get away with painting an idealised female (and male) nude.

No wonder this painting has always belonged to secular owners and ended up in the legendary *Vaults of Titian* (for a comment on the *Vaults of* Titian, please see *Venus and the Organist* by Titian in this guide) in Madrid alongside other works by Rubens, Tintoretto and Titian.

## Elements in the painting

*Adam and Eve* is presented as a diptych on two separate panels, both panels are roughly two metres in length. Both figures are also close to being life size and their proportions are clearly classical in their execution. Indeed, anyone who is familiar with classic Greek sculpture will easily note a resemblance between Adam's pose and the *Apollo Belvedere* sculpture (The *Apollo Belvedere* is possibly one of the classic sculptures that has epitomised ideals of aesthetic perfection in Western Europe since the Middle Ages). In the case of Durer's *Adam*, the weight of Adam's body falls on his left foot thus creating a classic downwards tilt of the hip on Adam's right side. You will always know you are contemplating a figure inspired in Greek classicism if you see this unmistakable tilt of the hip, in one direction or the other. Adam is also anatomically idealised following (again) Classic Greek aesthetics, with clearly defined muscles and an athletic body that is not too far off the mark of current male aesthetics. Perhaps more intriguing is *Eve*, as on the one hand, she appears to be almost as tall as Adam as well as also presenting a superb study in female anatomy. The size of Eve, much taller than the average female, is necessary to create a balance between the two figures.

The fact that Durer omitted any sort of background or detail in the paintings (except for the necessary tree of life and serpent in Eve's panel) is evidence that he was only interested in Adam and Eve's nude bodies.

## Why have I included this painting in this guidebook?

Bearing in mind that painting female nudes was difficult at the time, and the fact that Durer not only depicted a physically correct nude female body but that he also depicted an idealised sensual (if not sexual) nude female body (and got away with it!) is reason enough to make the cut for this guide.

## Durer

Durer is considered one of the greatest artist in northern Europe during the Renaissance. Indeed, there is no other artist at the time in Germany who would have the impact that Durer had. A true man of the Renaissance, he was not only a gifted painter and engraver but also an inspired mathematician and theorist. Durer was also very successful in his lifetime and even boasted the protection and patronage of Maximilian I, the Holy Roman Emperor at the time.

In line with other renowned artists at the time, it was thanks to visits to Italy that would mark the turning point in their careers and provide them with the necessary exposure to revolutionary Renaissance ideas that would transform their styles. Durer was no exception and the two trips he made to Italy had a profound influence on his work (*Adam and Eve* are clear examples of this).

However, what I have always found much more interesting about Durer were his business skills. Durer was possibly just as much an entrepreneur as he was an artist. In fact, despite enjoying Imperial patronage, he steered away from courts and royal appointments remaining economically independent throughout his life (this was very unusual back in the 16th century). He was able to do this because he sold prints (woodcuts or engravings). Prints are an artist's financial dream as they allow multiple reproductions of the same image. In other words, they are an affordable way for one work of art to be reproduced hundreds of times and then sold a lot cheaper than a painting. Furthermore, Durer was most likely better known for his engravings in Europe than his paintings. These would reach astronomical prices putting them out of the reach of the middle and lower classes.

## 16th century pirating and copyrights

In this manner, demand for his engravings was large enough for other engravers to copy and reproduce his engravings selling them at a fraction of the cost (what we would call nowadays a *Durer knockoff*). In an attempt to safeguard the rights of his own work, Durer not only created (possibly) the first copyright logo in history: his famed signature composed of an A and a D, but also at least in one occasion took other engravers to court for plagiarism. Unfortunately for Durer, the court ruled in favour of the other artist as long as they did not incorporate Durer's signature in the copied engraving. This sentence clearly did not satisfy Durer who would include the following colophon (or copyright) in later works:

*Printed at Nuremberg by the painter Albrecht Dürer in the year Fifteen*
*hundred and twenty-one*
*Woe to you, ambusher of other people's labour and talent. Beware of laying your*

*rash hand on our work. Know you not what the most glorious Roman Emperor*
*Maximilian has conceded to us? - that no one shall be allowed to*
*re-print these pictures from spurious blocks, nor sell*
*them within the imperial realm. And if you do*
*so, through spite or covetousness, not*
*only will your goods be confiscated,*
*but you will also find yourself*
*in the greatest*
*danger.*

## 2. The Triumph of Death by Bruegel

Bottom floor - Room 56 A – Route A

## What's the picture about?

At first glance the *Triumph of Death* could be interpreted as an allegory of the transience of human life and the inevitability of death (note how even the rich and powerful succumb to death). It could also belong to the category of moralising paintings that explicitly represent the horrors of damnation for unrepentant sinners. However, if you look again, it appears that not only is no one getting saved in the picture but that Death has decided to come in the guise of an army of skeletons who in turn appear to be quite good at imitating human brutality when it comes to killing.

This leads me to believe that what we are contemplating is an unconventional and allegorical representation of war (and not Death). Indeed, the skeletons present themselves as a single army, which has already devastated the towns in the background and has started its terror spree in the foreground. Likewise, the skeletons are indulging themselves in all manner of acts of humanlike violence, torture and murder. And what's Bruegel's final message after all this destruction and death? That there is no escape once caught inside the machinery of war; that the skeletons represent the warring armies that desolated Europe at the time.

This pessimistic point of view offers a hint of irony as the skeletons flaunt the Christian cross. It appears that Bruegel believes that once the violence starts, not even faith or religion can assist and there is no hope of salvation to a better world.

If you are familiar with Bruegel's work, you may agree that this painting is a sort of nightmare version of the same placid Flemish landscapes inhabited by carefree peasants that are common themes in his paintings.

**Elements in the painting**

The picture depicts a nightmare scenario in typical cartoonlike Flemish style where a vast army of skeletons is not only torturing and slaughtering the terrorised population but has completely laid waste to the countryside and towns.

The painting is roughly divided into a foreground where the main action is happening and the background where lots of things are happening too but depicted in less detail.

Starting from the background and moving forward there are several clouds of smoke suggesting burning towns, a couple of sunken ships, a homestead under siege, several skeletons cutting down trees, the corpses of livestock, and an army of humans outnumbered by two armies of skeletons. In the foreground there is an array of skeletons attacking everybody in sight while a huge army stands ready as the humans are herded into a boxlike container flanked with a cross and that has an uncanny resemblance to a train wagon (from a 21st century point of view). All this may have been familiar for Bruegel and the people from his time as civilians were usually caught in the middle of hostilities.

Methods of torture and murder are also illustrated in detail, such as (in the background) the odd looking poles with wheels, which were a popular form of torture and execution during the middle ages (people were tied to the wheels, all their limbs broken and then left to die slowly and rot in the air); or the beheading, the stabbing, two hangings, several deaths by drowning and a nude man being chased by hounds. The scene gets more graphic as you move forward where we can see, amongst other things, a baby being gnawed on by a dog next to her or his dead mother, a pilgrim getting his throat slit, several people being hauled away in a net, and several skeletons in disguise upsetting a feast (one is even groping a woman in distress) while another playfully joins the couple singing in the corner (Bruegel had a dark sense of humour).

The central part of the painting depicts the grim reaper on his horse, scythe in hand and accompanied by an army of skeletons who are easily killing any resistance while they horde the humans into the box. I love the skeleton with the drums on top of the box who is providing a soundtrack to the scene.

## Why have I included this painting in this guidebook?

Because Bruegel is one of the few painters that has deigned to illustrate the reality of war; that there is no honour or glory in the battle, just random violence and suffering. The fact that he ruled out any sort of redemption to salvation in the painting offers a disturbingly pessimistic and realistic view of human nature as a whole.

## Bruegel

Not much is known of Bruegel's life. As a 16th century Flemish artist, he was contemporary to Michelangelo and was born just after the deaths of Raphael and Leonardo da Vinci. However, he apparently expressed very little interest in revolutionary Italian Renaissance art, even after having travelled to Italy. If Italian Renaissance paintings lean towards the grandiose, with almost sculpture-like figures that appear to break out of their two-dimensional confinement, Flemish 15th and 16th century paintings are depicted almost as book illustrations.

Bruegel, as most Flemish painters at the time, appeared to have been more interested in the story being told rather than the technique employed. Indeed, he was allegedly nicknamed Bruegel the Peasant because he would frequently disguise himself as one and mingle at different celebrations and events where he could observe unobserved. In this manner, most of his paintings recreate everyday peasant life (albeit with an ironic touch) and his peasants are frequently simplistically represented and even anatomically incorrect at times.

## Bruegel and Bosch

Bruegel's *Triumph of Death* will undoubtedly remind you of Bosch's *Garden of Earthly Delights* (at least the panel describing Hell). Indeed, Bruegel doesn't have problems in admitting his admiration of Bosch. However, although using similar cartoonlike characters along with a morbid and vivid imagination when it comes to representing nightmare scenarios, Bruegel is much more literal and arguably easier to interpret. If Bosch falls within the realm of the surreal with his grotesque hellish creatures, Bruegel remains within the realm of the allegorical. Bruegel is moralising, he has point to make and he makes it, his skeletons kill like humans. His counterpart and countryman, Bosch, is much more cryptic, at times almost impossible to decipher.

## Conflict in the Netherlands in Bruegel's time

Bruegel lived during the wake of the most bloody and brutal moment in Dutch history. The Protestant Reformation was under full swing triggering the Wars of Religion and several Dutch provinces (mainly the Protestant ones) were just about to begin their wars for independence from Catholic Spain. This basically meant that the Netherlands felt the full force of the Catholic Counter-Reform led by Spain, who was not about to lose a large part of its kingdom. Historians have documented several hundred (if not thousand) Dutch who were executed for heresy (basically not being Catholic). Bruegel died in 1569, one year after the start of the Eight Years' War.

## 3. The Garden of Earthly Delights by Bosch

Bottom floor - Room 56 A – Route A

**What's the picture about?**

The left and right panels seem to be clear enough (Garden of Eden and Hell), but then we have the middle panel and things get confusing. Therefore, and as there isn't a consensus when it comes to interpreting this painting, I will describe a few of the more popular interpretations, and you can chose.

*The classic interpretation*

This is the one found in most art books. It describes a sequential narrative of the triptych, starting on the left and moving across. Indeed, this is how triptychs were usually *read* in the middle ages. So we would have the Garden of Eden on the left panel illustrating the creation of man and woman. Then in the middle we would have a symbolic illustration of sinful humans indulging in all sorts of censurable behaviours that would represent Earth, as we know it. And finally, after all the debauchery in the middle, we arrive to hell in the right panel where humans are being punished for their sins.

The main problem with this interpretation is that it omits or ignores dozens of symbols and metaphors that clearly appear to be indicating something else, such as why is everybody running around carefree and naked?, and where are all the children and elderly?

*The Adamite interpretation*

This lesser known interpretation suggests that Bosch was an active member of the heretical Adamite sect. The interpretation of the left and right panels would stay the same, however, the interpretation of the middle panel would change drastically. The middle panel would illustrate the Adamite belief of having regained here on earth the innocence lost in the Garden of Eden (Christians tend to liken lost innocence with lust). This would imply that Adamites believed that they were beyond the constraints of Christian morality (mainly sexual), which did not exist before eating the apple. Indeed, they had a reputation of freely enjoying (all together) their nakedness and sexuality.

The main problem with this interpretation is that it would imply that Bosch was indeed a member of this sect. Considering that heretics were burned at the stake, it would have been very bold for Bosch to openly display his heretic beliefs like this, especially in Catholic dominated Netherlands.

*The existentialist interpretation*

In my opinion this is the soundest one as it apparently interprets satisfactorily almost everything we are looking at. In summary, the side panels remain the same as in previous interpretations, and the middle panel depicts a hypothetical Garden of Eden that did not undergo the passage from the Genesis of the Fall; that is, we have to imagine that Adam and Eve did not eat from the apple and were never expelled from the Garden. Indeed, look at the horizon line on the panel on the left and how it continues in the middle panel, suggesting that we are looking at the same place. The Garden in the middle also closely resembles the Garden on the left.

Bosch is imagining what God had in mind at the time of Creation assuming everything had gone as planned on day zero. Or in other words, what would human existence have looked like if Adam had not eaten from the apple and had not sinned, and humans had simply reproduced like animals, following their instinct, devoid of lust. Indeed, the Bible quite clearly indicates the Lord's commandment to Adam and Eve, that they should be fruitful and multiply and replenish the earth. So in theory, God had reproduction in mind (and considering Adam's gaze in the left panel, so did he).

This would imply that humans would have continued living completely carefree in the Garden, enjoying their innocence, reproducing without shame and unaware of any sort of morality, as sin did not exist. In summary, the middle panel would depict the Garden of Eden (and by default Earth) by illustrating the hypothesis of: *what would Earth look like if Adam and Eve hadn't eaten the apple?*

But it's not only sexual reproduction that concerns Bosch. Humans trapped in the Garden of Eden with nothing to do meant that eventually something was bound to go wrong. So what Bosch is also saying is that no matter what humankind did, at some stage we would have eventually fallen and been expelled from Eden; because to fulfil the command to multiply, humans would have eventually desired, which would have degenerated into lust.

The main problem with this theory is that there are still no babies or children in the picture (although painful labour and childbirth came as a punishment after the Fall, so it's hard to know what God had in mind for Eve at the very beginning).

## Elements in the painting

There is so much going on in this painting that evidently it is impossible to describe it all here. Likewise, the interpretation of the different iconography and symbols depicted is frequently difficult or even impossible to decipher.

Here is a selection of some of the more unusual and ambiguous ones, or just the ones I like best:

*Left panel – Garden of Eden at Creation*

1. There is a duck like figure reading in the pond in the Garden of Eden (bottom right corner). I have no idea what this surreal image represents nor have I found a satisfactory answer (there were no books in Eden!).
2. Animals are already killing and eating each other, suggesting a flaw in Creation and a liberal interpretation by Bosch of the Bible.
3. Eve is flanked to her right with two rabbits, common symbols of fertility and concupiscence. You have to love all these rabbits in classic painting.

4.   The owl, a symbol of darkness and evil, already makes its first appearance in this panel, right in the middle in the Tree of Life. This does not seem very appropriate.

*Middle panel – Garden of Earthly Delights*

1.   In the background, in the round hole in the middle tower a man is clearly grasping (violently) a woman's private parts, this is clearly lust and not instinctive reproduction.
2.   Note how the men are segregated from the women in the middle pond. The men ride their animals showing off and doing acrobatics while the women look on, some even bored and another already leaving the pond. As there is no lust, this would just be playful fooling around about to go wrong.
3.   Note how the rider behind the white goat is clearly riding a phallic shaped beast and how several of the animals display swollen testicles.
4.   The majority of the fruit picking, eating and hugging were sexual metaphors at the time.
5.   My favourite image is the hidden couple making love inside the large mussel.
6.   In the bottom right hand corner there is a small cave; inside the only male wearing clothes (or he is just very hairy) is pointing at a pensive woman behind a glass shield. Behind him is another person in the cave. Once again I am clueless to what this little section is meant to represent.

*Right panel – Hell*

1.   Bosch does not include all seven deadly sins in his Hell; rather, he focuses mainly on the punishment of lust and greed (although there are lesser acknowledgments of vain and pride).
2.   The *Tree Man* in the centre of the painting may be a self-portrait of Bosch. If this were the case, he would have placed himself in the midst of Hell while he turns his head around to tell us something (something very sombre and possibly regretful as he looks straight at the spectator).
3.   In the bottom right corner the guy being kissed by a pig-nun may be a critical allusion to the commerce in Indulgences, popular at the time.

4. It is unclear what Bosch's issue with music and musical instruments were; possibly an allegory of the perversion of human creativity. However, their importance in the panel suggests that we are missing something here.
5. The large pink bagpipe is an obvious symbol of male sexual organs, in fact, the whole panel is obsessively populated with phallic and sexual symbols.
6. Finally, another of my favourites, right below the knight being devoured and the large knife is a soldier with spurs who is riding a female as if she were horse. Besides the bestial lust this depicts, it is a rare commentary of the subjugation of woman in medieval society.

## Why have I included this painting in this guidebook?

Because it is one of the most iconographic art images of all times, one that almost anyone immediately recognises. To an extent, this painting has transcended its artistic condition and has now become a social icon.

And, from a personal point of view, the provocative ambiguity, the openness to interpretation and the surrealist irony are all elements that enhance art appreciation.

## Bosch

Little is known of him or his life apart that he was born in present day Netherlands (a part of the kingdom of Spain then) and that he died in 1516. The little information that has reached us comes from registers or notes found in the municipal records of his hometown and the local lay religious group *Brotherhood of Our Lady*, which he belonged to.

We also know that he was successful during his lifetime and that his work continued to be highly appreciated and imitated after his death. One of his more important enthusiasts would be the Spanish King Philip II who purchased posthumously several of his better-known paintings.

## 4. Portrait of Philip II by Anguissola

Bottom floor - Room 56 – Route A

**What's the picture about?**

The painting is a portrait of the King of Spain Philip II.

**Elements in the painting**

This is a classic portrait with Philip II facing the spectator and depicted waist upwards. In line with the style of the epoch, Philip II is dressed in solemn black. He is not wearing a crown and in his left hand he is holding a rosary. On his chest is the emblem of the Order of the Golden Fleece.

**Why have I included this painting in this guidebook?**

Because, like the painting by Gentileschi in this guide (see the chapter *Birth of Saint Jon the Baptist* by Gentileschi for more information), it was also painted by a woman and in the 16th century! That's a generation before Gentileschi started painting, making it even more remarkable.

I am aware that to have included a painting just because a woman painted it is to engage in debatable issues of positive discrimination. However, I believe that the fact that there are almost no female painters hanging in the museum (look around, I doubt you'll find the other two); that the painting was executed at a time when women's rights were virtually inexistent and apart from matrimony or the convent not much more was expected from them;

Furthermore, this painting has become overtime the unofficial *official* portrait of Philip II and perhaps the one that best describes his personality. Unsurprisingly, and like Gentileschi a generation after her, several of Anguissola's paintings, *Portrait of Philip II* included, were later attributed to male artists coetaneous to her.

### Sofonisba Anguissola

Sofonisba Anguissola was born into a noble family in Italy in 1532. Her father, for reasons unknown, decided to educate his six daughters in art. Out of the six, Sofonisba was undoubtedly the most accomplished one, achieving a reputation in Italy as a skilled portrait painter. A turning point in her artistic career may have been her trip to Rome at the age of 22 where she was introduced to Michelangelo and with whom she corresponded for several years. Although she did not train directly under Michelangelo, it appears that he offered on-going advice and guidance of her work through letters and sketches. However, Anguissola was never able to truly develop her skill, as apprentice positions at workshops (and therefore access to the study and observation of human anatomy) were vetoed to women (God forbid they see a nude man). This may be the reason she specialised in portraits, which do not require an in depth knowledge of the human body.

At the age of 26 she joined the Spanish Court as a lady-in-waiting and art tutor to Philip II's wife Elisabeth of Valois. Her skill and talent were recognised and she would eventually achieve court painter status. At the age of 39 Anguissola married a nobleman (who is said to have been supportive of her painting) and after several years in Madrid they moved to Palermo where her husband died a year later, in 1579. That same year Anguissola met her second husband who apparently was considerably younger than her. After getting married in 1580, the couple moved to Genoa where Arguissola continued painting in her own studio, eventually becoming a patron of the arts and receiving colleagues and admirers of her work (the renown painter Van Dyck was amongst them). She died at the age of 93 in Palermo.

## Female painters in the Prado

There are usually only three female painters exhibited in the Prado: Sofonisba Anguissola, Artemisia Gentileschi and Clara Peeters.

Two have made the cut for this guide and information can be found in their respective chapters. 17th century Peeters is mainly known for her still life paintings (the depiction of food and everyday objects, usually without humans), which I have always found to be of little interest.

## Spanish Habsburg fashion

One thing that draws people's attention when facing this painting is the King's royal attire. Here is Philip II, possibly the most powerful European monarch of his time without a crown or a sceptre and dressed in plain black. However, at the time, this was the fashion for the aristocracy and nobility, which considered black as being stylish and elegant. The flare, glitter and bling would have to wait until the Bourbon dynasty from France introduced their own French aristocratic fashion (as you admire the different portraits in the Prado, you can probably tell who was Habsburg and who was Bourbon just by the clothes they are wearing).

In any case, Philip II and the rest of the Habsburgs after him liked their black and dark colours. It went well with the conservative, pious, solemn and stiff-necked reputation they wanted to convey (indeed, the starched high collars gave the wearer no option than to walk around literally with their necks very erect). It was almost as if the Spanish ruling class were expressing the idea that they had more important things on their mind than bother with fashions, wardrobes and overt displays of power and wealth. And even visitors from abroad when admitted to court were advised to change into suitable plain and dark clothes so as not to offend.

What is interesting is how the Fundamentalist Catholic Habsburg's sworn enemies, the fundamentalist Protestant insurgents in the North, would appropriate Habsburg fashion to the extent that we cannot conceive Luther, Calvin or Zwingli if not in black. Perhaps there is an association between religious fundamentalism and dark colours.

## Philip II

The King of Spain Philip II reigned between 1556 and 1598. He was the son of the Emperor Charles V, whom he succeeded as King of Spain when his father abdicated. He could have been crowned, like his father, Emperor of the Holy Roman Empire, but his Spanish upbringing and the stronger political position of the future Ferdinand I (his uncle and Charles V's brother) led Philip II to not pursue this possible claim. Philip II did however inherit a huge empire that included vast amounts of European territories and everything discovered and conquered across the Atlantic Ocean.

Philip II was a warring monarch and literally picked a fight on every border of his empire. He fought, amongst others, the Dutch insurgents in the Netherlands, the Protestants in current Germany, the Portuguese in Portugal and the Turks in the East Mediterranean. He also fought the English in his much-ridiculed attempt to invade England with his Great Armada. Clearly all these wars cost money leading Philip II to declare bankruptcy four times during his regency.

However, Philip II is also considered the greatest of the Habsburg monarchs to rule Spain and it was during his reign when the Spanish Empire would reach its pinnacle through war and political intrigues (mainly marriages and claims). During his reign, Philip II would also be crowned King of England through marriage with Mary I of England (who died without offspring) and King of Portugal through a claim to the Portuguese throne becoming without doubt the most powerful European monarch of his time.

The pious Philip II is also the same person who commissioned the naughty themed paintings from Titian (see the chapter *Venus and the Organist* by Titian for more information) and others, as well as having his own private viewing room for these paintings.

## 5. Hare Hunt by Anonymous (Romanesque painting)

Bottom floor - Room 51 C – Route A

### What's the picture about?

The painting depicts a hare hunt. However, if we consider that this image was painted on the wall of a medieval church and that it does not represent a religious subject, then this hunting scene must surely have another meaning.

First of all, hunting (hares or other animals) was an activity the people of the time could easily relate to, although most likely the majority could not practice it as both the animals and the sport were usually reserved for the ruling elite. But that does not change the fact that your average peasant could look at the wall and say to himself: that's a man on a horse hunting hares with his dogs. The next step would be for that same peasant to ask himself if the scene is telling him something else (you will excuse me for using the generic *he*).

In this manner art historians have suggested that the hunting scene may really be representing an allegorical *divine* hunting scene in which the hares represent human souls. Hares were traditionally symbols of concupiscence (sexual desire) and feeble spirits in general. So in this case, the hares would represent us sinners, victims of our own nature and the divine hunt with Christ symbolised as the hunter would eventually catch us and save our souls. The fact that there are three dogs is also interesting (three is an important number in Christian numerology); the fact that there are two hares may allude to man and woman.

So perhaps what the local priest may have been trying to convey is that there is no escape.

## Elements in the painting

There is a hunter mounted on his horse holding a trident in his right hand. In front of him are three hunting dogs that are superimposed so as to suggest depth and ahead of them are two hares running into a net set in the last tree. The only suggestion of a landscape or setting for the hunt are the three trees that frame the image on both sides and separate the hunters from the hunted. Surprisingly, this economy in elements and simplicity in the composition is all the artist needed for the viewer to see a hare hunt in a forest. There is absolutely nothing else to divert the viewer from the simple but direct message.

## A crash course in Romanesque art

Romanesque art roughly corresponds to the period in Europe between the 10th and 13th centuries. Most Romanesque art presents similar characteristics making it very easy to discriminate. Unsurprisingly the *Hare Hunt* complies perfectly with these general characteristics:

1. The figures in the scene are depicted in size according to their importance (the hares must be important as they are obviously disproportionate to the rider and the hounds).
2. The figures, although depicting a chase, are rigid and appear to be frozen in the air. The artist just wanted us to *read* movement, not to actually depict it.
3. There is no emotion that can be read. No, that is not a hint of a smile on the hunter.
4. There is no need or care for tridimensionality or depth. Colours are flat and backgrounds tend to be monochrome.

## Why have I included this painting in this guide?

The simplicity of Romanesque art has always fascinated me, possibly because of the contemporary feel that these pictures have. The conceptual and symbolic nature of these paintings describe a surprising parallelism with 20th century art styles, which tend to flee from realism and naturalism. Or in other words, what is important is the message conveyed and not the skill and technique through which it is conveyed.

This does not mean that the painting becomes simplistic in its narrative, indeed, Romanesque paintings can become quite complex in their apparent simplicity; it does mean however that to interpret the painting, an effort must be made by the viewer, sometimes not always possible if there are elements or components alien to the current viewer. Likewise, the ambiguity of the narrative and the iconography for contemporary viewers that do not have access to medieval narrative is almost disconcerting. This in itself is another incentive, as the interpretation almost becomes a puzzle or game that beckons a solution.

## The pillaging of San Buadelio de Berlanga

The *Hare Hunt* is just one of the frescoes that graced the inside of the church of San Baudelio de Berlanga. Like all medieval churches, San Baudelio's walls and ceiling was completely covered with brightly coloured frescoes on the inside (and most likely on the outside as well). In fact, San Baudelio is considered one of the best examples of Romanesque art that has reached us. However, if you look around you, you will note that the Prado only has six frescoes even though all of the frescoes were removed from the church at the beginning of the 20th century.

So where are these frescoes and how did they get there?

They are now spread out in three different museums in the United States and here in the Prado; and the ones in the States are there because they were irresponsibly sold to an American art dealer at the beginning of the 20th century. Furthermore, the Prado only has six frescoes because 30 years later Spain exchanged the frescoes from the apse of another Romanesque church for them.

Thank goodness these dealings all belong to a darker age in Spanish history when naivety, corruption and plain ignorance led to the pillaging of priceless works of art.

So, if you are ever in New York, Boston or Indianapolis, you can continue your visit of the San Baudelio frescoes.

## The anonymous medieval artist

We do not know the name of the artist (or artists) that completed the frescoes in San Baudelio, nor do we know the name of any artist from Romanesque times (and only a handful from the Gothic period that followed the Romanesque).

In our current 21st society this may be difficult to understand as artists have come to represent the embodiment of human ego and vanity. However, in the Middle Ages things were a bit different. If you were a painter of frescoes, it most likely meant that your father was or had also been a fresco painter (and if you were a shoemaker, your father was probably one too). In this manner you would have been trained as an apprentice in a fresco painter guild, by your father or by another master in the craft.

And that was what art was considered back in the Middle Ages, a craft that was supervised by the local guild. And you could be more skilled or less skilled, but you worked with your hands to make a living and were a craftsman or an artisan. There might have been some prestige if you were good enough and possibly the different churches and monasteries might have sought your talent, but you would socially never be more than the lower working class in society. So, if you were *nobody*, you obviously could not sign your work, just like a basket weaver does not sign his baskets.

This is clearly light years away from the social status and almost celebrity recognition many current artists enjoy.

## 6. The Dog by Goya

Bottom floor - Room 67 – Route A

## What's the picture about?

The fact that the dog appears to be trapped or sinking into the ground is in itself disturbing. Likewise, the fact that Goya uses a dog is also disturbing (a dog as a possible metaphor of us humans?). The grimy void in the background, which does not represent anywhere in particular, becomes a threat as it looms vertically over the dog; almost helping to bury the animal with its weight. This oppressive vertical composition is clearly intentional and the void/sky/background is an effective and disturbing presence in the painting. We will never know what Goya meant exactly when he painted this picture (nor the rest of the *Black Paintings*), although it is unlikely that Goya had a specific story in mind. In my opinion (and other's), Goya culminated his need to express concepts such as pessimism, nihilism, futility and emotional fatigue that he was suffering at the end of his life. All of this is what I see when facing *The Dog*. However, it is an ambiguous painting open to many interpretations; and I am sure that every single viewer sees something similar, but different.

These are all concepts common to current contemporary art and clearly Goya was years ahead of his time as this painting could easily be signed and appreciated by any current contemporary artist.

## Elements in the painting

*The Dog* is one of the recovered frescoes from Goya's last residence in Madrid and possibly the most intriguing of the *Black Paintings*. The painting depicts a dog that appears to be almost buried with only his head showing as it looks upwards. The background is a light dirty ochre colour while the dog seems to be buried or sinking into a darker coloured terrain. And that's it. If it was not for the identifiable head of the dog, we could easily be contemplating a 1940s expressionist abstract art painting.

## Why have I included this painting in this guidebook?

Because Goya has taken ambiguity to the extreme. And this is probably why most people, myself included, find this painting fascinating and a bit disturbing, as there is no theme to relate to.

The other frescoes in the Black Paintings collection appear to have a theme, albeit at times not easily recognisable or interpretable. But in the case of the *The Dog*, there is nothing else but the buried/sinking dog and a vast void behind it. Goya has dispensed with any imagery or symbolism that can help us interpret the painting. It is almost as if he has taken the final step in western art and does away all together with the need for a story or a narrative for the painting. Goya, perhaps unintentionally as the painting was not meant to be viewed by the public, produced a painting that calls for a new language to decipher it, not one that we are accustomed to that is based on a narrative and the interpretation of the different pictorial elements in the painting.

In *The Dog*, Goya expects us to read an emotion through colour and composition. And I doubt anyone perceives a happy emotion here.

## Goya's Black Paintings

A note must be made on the whole series of *Black Paintings* as, although each one is a masterpiece in its own right, they are all part of a series and as such should be contemplated and admired.

The series was apparently painted sometime around 1820 when Goya was around 75 years old. All the paintings are frescoes (paintings painted directly on walls) that were salvaged, restored and transferred to canvases and framed in 1874. It is hard to tell to what extent the frescoes were damaged during this process although there is evidence that some of the paintings were altered significantly (ie. the two men fighting with clubs were not originally buried to their knees, this was added later once on canvas to perhaps fix a mess up of the process). In any case, the frescoes were painted on the walls of Goya's residence on the outskirts of Madrid where he was living at the time known appropriately as the *Quinta del Sordo* (*Villa of the Deaf Man*, although it was nicknamed after its previous owner and not Goya who was also deaf at the time). They were also painted as a personal whim and not by commission or to be exhibited in public. There is reason to believe that the walls of the house had already been decorated with lively rural scenes, some of which were used as backgrounds for these frescoes. After leaving Spain to France where Goya spent the last years of his life, he left the property to his grandson, who then sold it to a wealthy French banker, who in turn would donate the paintings to the Prado (before demolishing the house).

When Goya painted the *Black Paintings* he had already survived two nearly fatal illnesses, a war and was deaf. Historians like to believe that this cocktail of age, disenchantment with life and the world and possibly clinical depression led to the creation of this series. The disturbing themes and imagery appears to support this theory. In this manner, apart from *The Dog,* there are also, amongst others, a gathering of witches presided by a he-goat (Satan?), a painting of the fates (Atropos ready with her scissors), a very evil looking religious procession (in honour of Madrid's patron saint), Saturn devouring his son (disturbingly gory), or an elusive painting of two women laughing with a man who appears to be masturbating (this last detail conveniently left out in most guidebooks).

# Goya

Unlike other court painters in Spanish art history (such as Velázquez), Goya did not have a meteoric career. He did not become an official painter at the court of Charles III until he was 43 years old; and it would not be until the reign of Charles IV, two years later when he would finally achieve official court stardom. Clearly it was not a good idea to have clashed with Mengs, whom he studied under during his apprenticeship in Madrid and who was at the time the most important painter at the Spanish court. He was also denied twice membership to the Royal Academy of Fine Arts in Madrid. You have to admit that Goya was not only a bit rash (it's usually a bad idea to fall out with your instructor, especially if he is the big honcho in town) but also very ambitious as he sat both examinations before the age of 21. Realising his career was going nowhere he left Madrid and spent some time in Italy. It would take over 20 years (during which 5 were spent preparing simplistic paintings and sketches to be used on tapestries), a development of his artistic aptitudes and more importantly, the required intercession of powerful friends for him to gain admittance to the court and royal recognition.

Goya is renown for both his paintings and his engravings. Perhaps it is in the latter where the genius of Goya is best observed as he would have been less constrained and was able to give free reign to his more critical and subversive nature (the series on the brutality of war is probably just as moving today as it was 200 years ago). Indeed, it is in the Goya working for his own pleasure where he becomes one of the great masters in European art and not just another talented court painter.

## 7. Fable by El Greco

Top floor - Room 8 B – Route A

### What's the picture about?

No one is really sure what Greco meant to depict in this enigmatic painting. What we do know is that the subject fascinated El Greco who painted two other copies of the same theme.

A possible interpretation is that the painting is an illustration of a popular Spanish saying from the time with a moralising message: *Man is fire, woman is tow, and the devil comes and blows.* In this manner, the painting would be an allegory of the inherent sexual risk that too much familiarity between opposite sexes can have. Apparently human nature is much too fragile, and when a man and woman are together anything can happen. This interpretation makes sense as monkeys frequently symbolize sexual vice, the man has a silly grin and they are all in trance as they gaze into the kindled flame (flame as lust is another classic metaphor). Evidently, it is the woman who is guilty in this case of sparking the flame of lust. The moralising message would be to take caution against the base and possibly foolish instinct of lust.

However, in the other two versions of this painting that were painted previous to this one, the figure in the middle is definitely a young boy and not a girl. Furthermore, there is also a painting by Greco of just a boy lighting a candle with an ember without the monkey and the man. All of this suggests that El Greco did not change the sex of the middle person in the last version he painted (this one) but that indeed it is still a young boy. If this were the case, then the interpretation of the painting gets a bit muddled as we would have a naughty monkey and two men, one young and another definitely middle-aged. Perhaps El Greco is alluding to the fact that lust is sparked as easily at all ages; or perhaps there is a hidden homosexual component.

## Elements in the painting

A chained monkey and a man with a red hat are grouped around a young girl (or boy) who is lighting a candle with an ember. The man with the red hat is grinning and the monkey is observing the flame in interest. The background is dark because of the contrast with the light from the candle. This dramatic chiaroscuro technique (use of strong contrasts between light and dark for dramatic effects) used by El Greco was revolutionary in the sense that it predates by several years Caravaggio, the master of chiaroscuro.

## Why have I included this painting in this guide?

Because the enigmatic *Fable* stands out in its apparent simplicity and intimacy from the rest of El Greco's monumental paintings that are found in The Prado.

I will admit that I am not a huge fan of El Greco or of the succession of portraits and uncanny spiritualised religious paintings that he is better known for. However, the enigma that shrouds the *Fable* has made it one of my preferred paintings in the museum.

## Animals as metaphors and symbols in European art

If you see an animal in a painting, it is probably there for reason. Animals have almost always been depicted in paintings as symbols that represented something else. However, animals could symbolise different things as well and it depended on the subject and the rest of the elements in the painting to decipher the meaning of the animal. Interpreting the meaning of animals was not a cause for concern for artists as the codes for these symbols were widely understood (just like the codes for traffic sign symbols are almost automatically interpreted correctly by the majority of us).

In the case of the *Fable*, I have already alluded to the symbolism of the monkey. Here are a few more:

Dogs: Usually associated with fidelity and loyalty. If there is a dog near or with a woman, you can be sure that she is faithful to her husband.

Rabbits: Also usually associated with fertility and promiscuity. A rabbit or two in a painting indicates that there is room for a bit of a romp.

Pelicans: Almost always associated with charity. Apparently medieval Christianity believed that mother pelicans would go so far as to wound themselves in the breast so as to feed their young.

Peacocks: Associated with immortality. For some reason medieval Christianity believed that the flesh of peacocks did not decay after death.

Cats: Unexplainably associated with evil. This may have been because of a cat's independent nature, rejecting obedience (like dogs), even when domesticated.

Lions: Always associated with strength, courage and elegance. It also represents Christ's resurrection, as lions were believed to sleep with their eyes open.

Bears: Usually associated negatively with concepts such as violence, pride and cruelty. When depicted fighting it represents the struggle between good and bad.

Snake: This one does not need any explanation; it's had a bad reputation since day one on earth.

# El Greco

El Greco roughly translates as *The Greek*; and this gives us some clues about his origin. His real name was Doménikos Theotokópoulos (clearly the Spaniards found his nickname a lot easier to remember and pronounce) and he was born in 1541, just after the first classical wave of Renaissance art in Italy (think Raphael and Michelangelo). Before coming to Spain with the aim of becoming a court painter at Philip II's court, El Greco learnt the profession in Crete and later in Venice and Rome. However, and after failing to impress Philip II, El Greco would take up residence in Toledo where he would spend the last 26 years of his life till his death in 1614 achieving both fame and notoriety. In this manner, El Greco has come to be known as a Spanish master.

El Greco, is also one of those odd cases in art history where it is virtually impossible to allocate him to any conventional art school of his time. His eccentric style seems to fall within the mannerist movement, however, a quick inspection of other mannerist painters from his time will quickly dismiss this theory (eg. Tintoretto or Bronzino). Clearly El Greco was ahead of his time and until the early 20th century there hasn't been an artist that vaguely resembles his style. What is more, and this is what I find most impressive about the man, he got away with it, even after being rejected by Philip II. Perhaps his style was disdained after his death, nor was he imitated in life, but he managed to succeed in Toledo and was commissioned work in all the major churches and monasteries till his death; and as I mentioned previously, 400 years later his legacy would make an impact on European art at the end of the 19th and beginning of the 20th century.

But perhaps the facet of El Greco that is least known was his belief in himself and his style that may have bordered arrogance. As an example, he assumedly said of the late Michelangelo that *"he was a good man, but he did not know how to paint"* and then offered the current pope to paint over the last Judgment in the Sistine Chapel.

As a final note, El Greco's unconventional painting style was mirrored to an extent in his private life. He apparently had only one son out of wedlock with his companion Miss Jerónima de las Cuevas, whom he never married but with whom he lived. For someone as religiously oriented as he apparently was and who worked incessantly for the Catholic Church, this would have been highly unusual at the time; remember that the Spanish Inquisition was in full force.

## 8. Venus and the Organist by Titian

Top floor - Room 8 B – Route A

### What's the picture about?

Titian painted five different paintings with roughly this same motif; that is, a nude woman facing the viewer lying on a bed.

In an attempt to avoid more obvious interpretations, art historians have liked to describe these paintings as allegorical paintings with Venus. In this manner the painting has been described as a: '... *neoplatonic allegories of the senses, in which vision and hearing are instruments for knowing beauty and harmony.*' I assume they mean that the organ player is enrapt with both the music he is playing as well as with the beauty of his surroundings. In my opinion these are feeble (and prudish) attempts to avoid tarnishing so-called high art with much more mundane interpretations. Or in other words, I believe that this painting is simply an evident objectified representation of female sexuality (or a woman depicted exclusively as an object to be enjoyed by males).

The fact that there are other series of similar paintings, but not painted for the same person, supports the theory that these paintings had a more functional (and naughty) nature. Indeed, these paintings, and others by other artists, were commissioned for private use and usually hung in bedchambers.

Remember that 16th century Europeans did not have the access or saturation of visually stimulating images that we have nowadays. Eroticism was much more subtle, both because of the impossibility to access large numbers and a variety of erotic imagery as well as because of the social and religious norms and laws prevalent at the time. In other words, people could be imprisoned, tortured or executed for behaviours that fell outside of the established codes of conduct.

**Elements in the painting**

The painting represents a nude woman, lying on a bed or couch and represented so as to display without any need of imagination her physical attributes. This in itself recalls current day glamour or erotic photography.

Nude women are a recurrent theme in classic art, usually within a mythological context. Thus, if you painted the birth of Venus, you had a pretext to paint a young beautiful nude woman as an allegory of whatever the story led to; and all mythological paintings were allegories of something. Surprisingly the church frequently turned a blind eye to these types of paintings, as long as there was a clear allegoric interpretation behind the scene (and nudity).

In the case of Titian's *Venus and the Organist*, this allegoric interpretation is not that clear. The painting presents us with a young sexualized woman, who apparently is Venus (other paintings in the series also include Cupid) as Venus frequently represented nude, young and beautiful (with a lovely 16th century hairstyle and jewelry). She is accompanied by her playful dog, which usually represents fidelity (so apparently, although exhibiting herself and in company of an admirer, she maintains herself distant and chaste); and then there is an organ player who is playing a tune while he dislocates his back as he turns almost completely around to get a better view of her. In the background there is a garden complete with a satyr fountain and possibly several allegorical motifs such as the pair of horses, the couple, the stag, the wolf and the peacock. However, none of these elements distract us from the Venus and her admirer.

# Why have I included this painting in this guidebook?

Because even though it's base and reproachable, men who like women still get a kick out of these pictures, just like they did 400 years ago. Heterosexual men have really not changed that much in 400 years regarding their neuronal activation mechanisms, which I confess is a bit sad.

Perhaps what is most surprising about this painting is that it was commissioned by the future king Philip II, who, not only had a reputation of being a no-funny-business man, but also was also extremely conservative in his religious points of view. The code word for these commissions and type of painting was *poesie* (yes, really). Goes to show that you can never tell.

Finally, and as you will also appreciate in other paintings in the museum (ie. *Three Graces* by Rubens), it is interesting to observe how beauty canons have changed over time. If she had had the luck (or bad luck) to have lived in our time, our Venus would probably now be on a diet and spending quality time at the gym.

## Titian

Titian is the great *lesser-known* Renaissance (16th century) painter. He was contemporary to Raphael and Michelangelo (and to Leonardo da Vinci for a while) and also Italian; and like them, achieved recognition and fame during his lifetime. However, Titian has always been a second runner up when it comes to gauging the Renaissance and art history in general. The reasons for this are unclear as his skill is unquestionable; he enjoyed Imperial patronage and recognition, and he is considered one of the most influential painters of his generation. Perhaps he simply doesn't have a Sistine Chapel (Michelangelo) or a Mona Lisa (Leonardo) to be remembered by in our collective conscious.

If Italian Renaissance painting is characterised by line and drawing (bold silhouettes and well defined forms), Venice and its painters (Titian included) was always more interested in colour. Indeed, Titian would not always prepare preliminary sketches on the canvases for his paintings but would apply the paint directly, correcting as much as necessary. This way of painting would become painfully slow and it would not be unusual for Titian to spend years completing one single painting (he tended to work on several at the same time).

This love and predominance for colour over line would produce paintings that were much more vibrant and visceral in contrast to the solemnity and monumentality of, for example, Michelangelo's work. Likewise, this love for colour defines perfectly Titian's sensual nature. Indeed, Titian is perhaps not only the most erotic painter of his time but can also boast a biography characterised by a love for life and its pleasures. Unsurprisingly, one of his best friends (and whom he immortalised in a famed portrait) was the acclaimed controversial poet, philanderer and pornographer Pietro Aretino, who holds the dubious honour of having written the first pornographic (not erotic) novel in European history.

**Vaults of Titian**

The Vaults of Titian was the name given to the rooms in the Habsburg Palace in Madrid where all the paintings with explicit female nudity were stored under lock and key so as to avoid contaminating unprepared and weak minds, and clearly to designate a place in the Palace where they could be enjoyed privately. Philip IV (the gentleman with 8 illegitimate children) was the king who organised these rooms with the help of Velázquez (yes, the artist). As the largest series was by Titian, these rooms came to be known as the Vaults of Titian.

Fate saved the majority of the paintings in this collection from both the fire that destroyed the Habsburg Palace and from the later Bourbon monarchs (specially Philip V and Charles III) who had greater issues with nudity and eroticism than their Habsburg counterparts. Charles III even toyed with the idea of destroying them all in an act of puritanism (thank goodness the court painter Mengs talked him out of it), and Philip V gave away several (now in other museums around the world) and finally stored them away again under lock and key. When these paintings finally made their way to the Prado museum in the 19th century, they were again exhibited in reserved rooms where they would not offend the unprepared and which required a permit.

Several of the paintings included in this guide were part of the Vaults of Titian collection, such as, Durer's *Adam and Eve* or Ruben's *Three Graces*.

## 9. The Meninas by Velázquez

Top floor - Room 12 – Route A

**What's the picture about?**

For many the greatest painting of all time, and yet it's subject is ambiguous. *The Meninas* was apparently commissioned by Philip IV although it's not clear if the king wanted a portrait of himself or of his daughter (I doubt he wanted a portrait of Velázquez). So what does Velazquez do? He brazenly paints a self-portrait under the premise that he is painting a portrait of the princess Margarita, who happens to be visiting Velazquez's workshop (although the room portrayed is not his workshop) and captures the precise moment that the king and queen arrive unannounced; perhaps even more surprising is that you (the viewer) are more or less standing where the king and queen are standing and therefore you would be seeing exactly what they saw. In other words, you are seeing a *snapshot* of an everyday scene at the palace.

There is no documentation regarding the king's reaction to the painting, however, the painting was kept and hung in the king's personal rooms (he must have had a sense of humour as well as granting Velázquez permission to depict him reflected in the mirror).

In my opinion this whole game of illusions was just a pretext for Velázquez to exercise his skill and technique in a display of technical mastery.

**Elements in the painting**

As mentioned previously, the painting depicts a group of people in the room where the most important characters are surprisingly relegated to a vague reflection in the mirror (the king and queen).

The prominent person in the painting is the Princess Margarita; then come her ladies in waiting (these are the famous *meninas*, hence the title, although for years it was referred to as *The Family*), her buffoons and her dog. There is a nun and a gentleman behind her who have been identified (with name and surname) as her *bodyguard* and *governess* (the nun). The gentleman at the back by the door is supposedly the queen's personal steward.

The scene can be described as follows: The princess and her escort have come to visit the workshop where Velázquez is working. At some point she has requested a glass of water, which one of the *meninas* has fetched and is just handing it to her. The king and queen have made a sudden appearance in the room (right where you are standing) and this is the precise moment when Velázquez takes his *snapshot* as several of the people in the picture are not aware of their presence (eg. the dwarf kicking the dog, the *menina* handing the Princess her water and the nun), while the rest have suddenly realised who has just come in (eg. the bodyguard and the female dwarf are just reacting, the other *menina* has had time to start a curtsey, the princess has just turned her head towards her parents and Velázquez has stopped painting). It is unclear what the queen's servant is doing at the far side of the room (if entering or leaving).

## Why have I included this painting in this guidebook?

Perhaps one of the most common reactions when facing *The Meninas* is a sensation of disappointment. Indeed, you have probably already seen other paintings in the museum, which you have enjoyed more; even Velázquez has other paintings that are far more entertaining than this one. So, what is the big deal about this one? And why do critics and historians rave so much about it?

*The Meninas* is not famous because of the theme but because of what Velázquez achieved technique-wise (same thing with Leonardo's Mona Lisa; everyone is thrilled about the lady and her smile and the painting's interest is in the background). To understand what I am talking about we have to rewind several hundred years, to medieval times, and western European painters' quest to imitate nature, and moreover, to give their paintings three dimensionality (depth and perspective). Remember that before photography, the only way to reproduce nature in two dimensions was by painting or drawing. And it took western painters hundreds of years to achieve this. They figured out fairly quickly how to draw proportions, so that men looked like men and horses like horses. They realised fairly quickly too that things in the distance appeared smaller, and they drew them smaller. But the pictures looked like cartoons, that is, they did not look *real*. Painters slowly began to understand that objects in the distance had to look a bit blurrier, less defined than the objects in the front.

It was Velázquez who finally got it right, who finally understood how our eyes *see* things; that when we look, we see everything in a blur, out of focus, except for the object we are actually looking at. And that the farther away the objects are from the place we are looking directly at, the more out of focus they become. This is how our sight works, and a painting that is able to reproduce this, will look *real*. Now look again at *The Meninas*. The scene you are looking at is exactly how Phillip IV and his wife would have seen it, but in real life.

After Velázquez, art in Europe would enter a long period of crisis until the invention of photography in the 19th century, thus forcing art to reinvent itself (what was the point of copying nature if anyone could take a photo?) with the impressionists and the rest of the avant-garde movements in the 20th century.

I also love the idea that Velázquez had the nerve and inspiration to paint a picture that does not fall into any classic genre and predates our *Instagram* inspired world by 400 years.

## Velázquez, royal administrator

In 1652 Velázquez, already court painter, was appointed *aposentador mayor*, which can be roughly translated as *royal administrator*. His responsibilities included firstly organising where and how people slept (the king included) and where and how court activities were held. You can imagine that the logistics required for this job would have been daunting, especially each time the king and his court decided to make a trip (provisions, route, safety, protocol, royal agenda, entertainment... and all with a budget in mind). Although this appointment meant a brilliant political career for Velázquez, the unhappy truth for us art enthusiasts is that it left almost no time for Velázquez to paint, which is a shame as he was undoubtedly at the pinnacle of his artistic career.

Likewise, it would have also been Velázquez who would have assumed the unofficial role of royal *confident* for Philip IV's multiple affairs and other whims. Considering that Philip IV had at least 8 extramarital children, Velázquez would have been kept quite busy.

## Velázquez, pure blood knight

Another element that calls our attention is the Red Cross of Santiago painted on Velázquez's chest. This cross was painted after the artist's death, assumedly by order of the king, as Velázquez was only awarded knighthood after his death in 1660. The fact that Philip decided to do this not only reflects the esteem he felt for the artist but also concluded once and for all two outstanding issues that haunted Velázquez throughout his life: whether he indeed was part of the Spanish nobility and whether painting was a philosophical career (meaning that Velazquez earned his living with his mind not his hands).

To be knighted a knight of the Order of Santiago you had to belong to the Spanish nobility (and to belong to the nobility you could not have tainted blood in your veins) and you could not make a living with physical work.

## Velázquez, slave owner

And to conclude, a short note on Velázquez's slave and apprentice Juan de Pareja. Velázquez would free him in 1650 and Pareja would continue a fairly successful career until his death in 1670. Apparently it was quite common for painters in Spain in the 17th century to have a slave or two (usually of Arab origin) in their workshops.

Santiago is a town you will immediately fall in love with. The historic quarter is small (but large enough to explore for several days), manageable and safe (no cars and very little crime if any). It has also been fairly untouched and when you walk through the streets and quiet allies you may feel like you have been transported back in time. Indeed, when I was reading 19th century Bazán's *Pazos de Ulloa*, part of which takes place in Santiago, her descriptions fit like a glove to my own observations of the town, more than a hundred years later.

## 10. The Three Graces by Rubens

Top floor - Room 29 – Route A

## What's the picture about

The Graces were the illicit daughters of Zeus and the ocean nymph Eurynome. Their names were Aglaia (radiance), Euphrosine (mirth) and Thalia (flowering), just in case you are looking for an unusual name for your daughter. In Classic mythology they are commonly referred to as the virgin deities of love, charm and all things pleasing and graceful, who lived with the gods and helped them have a good time and escape boredom. They have always been a favourite in classic mythology as they incarnate the *joie de vivre* (joy of living) without the sexual and/or narrative tension that can be found in other motifs such as Bacchus's romps.

Rubens presents us with the three young ladies who are having a bit of a laugh in Arcadia (a mythological region in ancient Greece where shepherds and nature lived in unspoilt harmony and beauty; a kind of paradise on earth). However, if we were not told that they are the three Graces, we would probably just take them for a group of young playful 17th century beauties. And this is exactly what Rubens had in mind as he adapted the classic mythological theme to suit his own interests (mainly the exaltation of what he considered to be the epitome of female beauty that most of his peers could relate to).

This painting was part of Ruben's private collection. It was sold to the Spanish king Phillip IV after his death. The painting was added to the collection of nudes and other deemed erotic paintings in the king's private collection known as the *Vaults of Titian*. It was later almost destroyed in the 18th century because of its exaggerated profane and sensual nature. Thankfully it was finally stored again in a room in the Prado with limited access along with other paintings from the royal collection depicting female nudes.

**Elements in the painting**

The Three Graces are presented in classical fashion with the middle one turned away from the viewer. They are framed by a tree on the left where they have left their clothes hanging on the upper branches (except for one transparent veil as modesty demands) and on the right by a fountain. Above them is a garland of red and white flowers. In the background is an imaginary landscape of Arcadia (painters did not leave their studios to copy nature until the 19th century) with some deer placidly grazing. All three bodies are illuminated from where the spectator is standing with an unidentified light source. All three figures are intertwined physically as they embrace each other and emotionally as the middle one and the one on the right sensually gaze at the one on the left who in turn returns their gaze.

In my opinion, the disposition of the Graces and specially their eye communication clearly indicates a veiled homosexual element to the painting (that and they having lost their clothes).

**Why have I included this painting in this guide?**

For the only reason that this painting has fascinated me since childhood. I am sure there is a Freudian theory that can explain this fixation.

## Ruben's wives

Rubens was married twice. His first wife was Isabella Brant who married Rubens when she was 18 years old and died from the plague when she was 34 years old (Rubens was 49). As Rubens apparently preferred them young, four years later he married 16-year-old Hélène Fourment when he was 53 (that's a shocking 37 year difference). Ruben's *Three Graces* was painted in 1639, one year before his death; the blonde Grace on the left is Hélène Fourment, at the age of 25. Both his wives may have modeled for him, although it was Hélène who would become his particular muse and the epitome of female beauty during the last years of his life. In later paintings he would also depict her as Venus at *the Judgment of Paris* (when Paris judged Venus to be the most beautiful of all the goddesses thus sparking the war of Troy). Clearly, Rubens was an incorrigible romantic, fathering eight children; the last one born eight months after his death.

## Rubens

The German born painter (although Belgium raised) Rubens died in 1640 at the age of 63 in the Belgium city of Antwerp (then part of Spain). During his life he was one of the most well-known and admired painters in Europe. Indeed, the demand for his work was so great that his workshop literally became a factory where paintings were produced almost in chain line guise (his apprentices would paint most of the picture imitating his style and he would correct and paint the difficult parts such as the faces).

He was a friend of Velázquez and was likewise favoured at the court of Philip IV, from whom did he not only receive regular commissions but also worked as a Spanish diplomat for the Kingdom of Spain.

## Cellulite and pale white skin

The Graces are the deities of everything pleasing, hence they themselves are also pleasing, both in their behaviour as well as there appearance. In this manner, artists have always used this subject as a pretext to represent the current epoch's idealisation of beauty. Rubens was no exception and what you are contemplating is the 17th century European ideal of female beauty. Rubens represented so well this ideal that he even unintentionally coined the current term *Rubenesque* when we refer to a plump and rounded female body shape.

However, the 17th century was just as strict regarding ideal female body shapes as our current 21st century is. Hips, thighs and bosoms had to be ample and full, buttocks fleshy, rounded oval faces with a hint of a double chin, full stomachs, arms thick and shoulders broad (you get the idea). However, although round and plump (even a bit of cellulite was OK) was the beauty ideal in the 17th century (and 18th and 19th too), morbid obesity and lack of proportion was not. Body parts and flesh could be exuberant but never sagging or flabby. And this is what you see in the *Three Graces*, three women who portray health, sexual ripeness and prosperity (unlike our current standards, lean sinewy people were associated with poverty and working classes, must have had something to do with access to food and lifestyles).

Then there was the skin, which had to be pale white. Therefore, if you could, you stayed indoors and away from the sun. And if you deemed your skin tone to dark, then there was an amalgam of concoctions and makeups that would help to achieve the desired effect. As an example, 17th century women were fascinated with the properties of ceruse (lead based) and mercury as whiteners. In other words, these ointments not only had progressive abrasive properties on the skin (eventually deforming the skin completely) but also eventually led to poisoning and death if used in excess. It appears that beauty has always had a price, in 17th century Europe women did not have to starve themselves to be beautiful but ended up poisoning themselves.

## Cancer and rheumatism

Thanks to Rubens's love of realism, medical specialists have apparently found two disturbing elements in the *Three Graces*.

Firstly, the model for the Grace on the right may have been suffering from breast cancer. The model apparently has an open ulcer suggested by the reddening of skin, nipple retraction and a reduction of her breast volume as well as axillar lymph nodes. All of these physical symptoms may suggest a locally advanced breast cancer.

As for the rheumatism, there appears to be evidence that the model on the left (most likely his wife Hélène) may have been suffering severe rheumatoid arthritis. Rubens, a master in human anatomy would not have painted the awkward hand and fingers unless he intended to. Or in other words, Rubens probably painted the hand and fingers exactly as he saw them: deformed and with the characteristic 'swan's neck' or 'buttonhole' deformities of the fingers that are representative of this disease. Apparently, Rubens also suffered from gouty rheumatism, which disabled him at times leaving him bed-ridden.

## 11. The Story of Nastagio Degli Onesti, Part 1 by Botticelli

Bottom floor - Room 56 B – Route B

### What's the picture about?

The first thing you will have noticed is that this is one painting of a series. So what you are contemplating is the first part of a story depicted in almost cartoon likeness that is read sequentially.

The second thing you will have noticed is the graphic and sadistic violence depicted in all of the panels. The fact that this apparent random violence is directed towards a helpless and vulnerable woman makes the painting(s) even more disturbing to a contemporary viewer.

*The Story of Nastagio Degli Onesti, Part 1* as its name indicates is the first sequence of the whole story of Nastagio Degli Onesti. And the story of this gentleman belongs to the 8th story of the 5th day of the Decameron by Boccaccio (that's the medieval book about ten refugees telling each other stories, ten for each day making a 100 in total). So what you are looking at is the illustration of a fairly popular story in the 14th and 15th centuries (clearly times have changed). And the story goes as follows (starting with Part 1 and work your way to Part 3; unfortunately part 4 is in Italy):

The suitor Nastagio degli Onesti has left his friends and heartbroken walks through the woods near Ravenna (Italy) after the daughter of a nobleman has cruelly and arrogantly rejected his courtship. While in the woods he runs into a naked and dishevelled damsel in distress shrieking for mercy who is being pursued by a knight on horseback and his hounds. The knight eventually strikes her down (Part 2) and then proceeds to cut out her heart and some other organs and feed them to his dogs. The dead woman then gets up as if nothing had happened and both knight and hounds start the chase again. We then discover that these are the spirits of a dead couple condemned to all eternity to carry out this macabre hunt. The knight, like Nastagio, was a rejected suitor who committed suicide and the hunted woman was the lady who had rejected him and then gloated over his death. As the hunt apparently happens every Friday in the same spot, Nastagio organises a banquet and invites a bunch of people, his beloved amongst them (Part 3). And just as the banquet is at its best, along comes the hunt and frightens everyone into submission, mainly the lady he was wooing. She is so afraid to end up like the woman in the hunt that she accedes to Nastagio's desires and marries him; and they live happily ever after (Part 4, not in the Prado).

So I guess that the moral of the story is that if you were a female in the late Middle Ages and you rejected a suitor (thus showing a degree of independence and free will), you would be divinely punished to be tortured, symbolically raped and murdered throughout eternity; or you could accept a coercive marriage and submit your self and your body to your (male) suitor's will. More sympathetic art critiques may see an allegory of how excessive passion is just the reverse side of cruelty and hatred (even so, I am sure this idea could have been illustrated differently).

Note that all the women at the banquet (Part 3) look uncannily like the woman who is being hunted. This might imply that all women were collectively implicated and all women could be potential victims of male biased justice.

### Elements in the painting

*The story of Nastagio Degli Onesti, Part 1* takes place in a cartoon like world (bold outlines and everything represented in detail). Nastagio is the chap in the becoming red tights that must have been the quintessence of fashion at the time. He is painted three times in the same painting suggesting different moments of the story: First he is in the background chatting with his friends near the tents, then we see him strolling through the forest and finally we see him trying to ward off the dogs with a stick (if you were not familiar with the story you would probably think he is attacking the lady too). This is a classic medieval procedure for describing sequential events in a painting.

Then there is the hunt frozen just when the hounds catch their prey and the knight is about to smite her down. As modesty demands, the woman's nudity is somewhat hidden by a white cloth that covers her private parts.

Perspective (the eternal headache for late Gothic and early Renaissance painters) is achieved by reducing the size of the trees and figures, thus creating a suggestion of depth and three dimensionality.

### Why have I included this painting in this guide?

Because it may be one of the most controversial paintings in the whole museum. Indeed, I have seen more than one tourist briefly stand in front of it and react almost in shock or repulsion as the theme depicted is unimaginable for our current standards.

### A wedding gift

All four paintings were commissioned as a wedding gift by Lorenzo de Medici. I am sure the groom and his friends all had a good laugh at the time and the bride and her bridesmaids probably understood the (not so hidden) meaningful life lesson.

### The Decameron and Boccaccio

The Decameron is one of the great works of literature of all time. Written in the 14th century by the Italian author Boccaccio, the Decameron is a collection of 100 tales told by 10 people during 10 days (similar to Chaucer's Canterbury Tales). The pretext is that a group of refugees from the plague that is assailing Florence, decides to escape boredom by telling each other tales. The finality of these tales are centered on satirical depictions of human nature (lots of sex and deceit) rather than moralising allegories. Indeed, several of the tales would not be culturally or socially acceptable nowadays.

## Sandro Botticelli

Botticelli was one of the great Italian early Renaissance masters who would bridge the final years between the medieval Gothic style and the full Renaissance, although never quite embracing Renaissance classicism fully (he was contemporary to Leonardo da Vinci and a comparison between the two evidences this).

He was born in Florence in 1445 and was successful during his lifetime. He is perhaps best known for one of the most iconic paintings of all times: The Birth of Venus (that's the one with a nude woman standing on a shell coming out of the ocean). Boticcelli is another great painter that was gradually forgotten over time until he was *rediscovered* in the 19th century, possibly becoming since then the best known of all the early Renaissance painters.

It appears that apart from the glamour and success offered by the Medici commissions, Botticelli was also a devout follower of the fanatical sect led by the charismatic preacher Savonarola. This following would lead him to allegedly destroy several of his own works in one of the routine *Bonfire of the Vanities* (burnings of books, objects and really anything that can lead to sin) that were popular amongst the sect. His affiliation to Savonarola's teachings (even after the preacher's death who in a twist of fate would end up hung and then burnt to ashes in his own bonfire) would eventually lead him to poverty towards the end of his life as he gradually gave up painting and social recognition.

However, Botticelli was also an incorrigible romantic who never married, as apparently the object of his desire was a married woman, the lovely Simonetta Vespucci who was at one time proclaimed as the most beautiful woman in Florence. There is an unconfirmed legend that Simonetta modelled for Botticelli and that the Venus in his *Birth of Venus* is actually Simonetta (and nude!). Unfortunately, there is no evidence that this was the case (it sounds highly unlikely). However, we do know that when Botticelli died he had asked to be buried at Simonetta's feet in the church where she was already buried, and that his wish was carried out.

## 12. The Descent from the Cross by Van der Weyden

Bottom floor - Room 58 – Route B

### What's the picture about?

The painting is a classic, albeit very crowded, representation of Jesus's descent from the cross as described in the Gospels. Jesus has been crucified on the Golgotha mount (where all crucifixions took place in Jerusalem, the skull and bones remind us of this fact) and is now dead. He is depicted here with a loincloth, his crown of thorns and the nail wounds on his feet and hands as well as the spear wound in his side. This painting was commissioned for an altarpiece and Van der Weyden in line with these instructions painted one of the most passionate and moving religious representations of all time.

Van der Weyden manages to convey the idea of overwhelming grief and tragedy with apparent simplicity, grace and serenity. There is no excess, the figures are mourning almost in silence while the virgin, who has collapsed contributes to theatrical pose of all the actors.

## Elements in the painting

The first thing we notice is the unusual shape of the painting and frame: an inverted *T*. *The Descent from the Cross* was the main part of an altarpiece and this shape was quite normal at the time in the Netherlands. This may have been because an inverted *T* allows the painter to emphasise the central part of the painting, usually Jesus crucified, and consequently the painter could also fit the cross in too. The cross is also a commonly depicted *T* shape, known as a *Tau*.

The second thing that comes to mind when viewing the painting is the number of people. There are 10 people that have somehow fit (and gracefully) into a very limited space. In fact, the space is so cramped that if some of the figures were to move their head or to stand up straight they would block the person behind them from our view. Have a look at the man at the top of the cross, who is cramped in the top section, as one of the nails he is holding is even escaping the physical space of the painting and overlying the painted frame. Van der Weyden emphasises the importance of the spatial relationship amongst the figures by putting a solid gold background (if there is no background, then we are forced to concentrate on the figures themselves).

But perhaps what has made this painting most famous is the number of relations and parallelisms that can be found that serve the double purpose of reiteration and balancing the whole composition. The Virgin Mary has fainted and you can see how her body duplicates her son's body (down to the outstretched arms), which is being taken off the cross. Mary Magdalene who is on the far right is bent forward in grief, mirroring John the Evangelist (in a red tunic) who is on the far left. These two figures form a sort of human parenthesis with which they frame the whole scene. There are more, but I believe these two examples are enough to get the idea.

The people depicted conform to standard representations of the crucifixion after Jesus's death as described in the Gospels. They are:

The Three Marys (Mary Cleophas, Mary Salome and Mary Magdelene) and the Virgin Mary (mother of Jesus). Mary Cleophas is the woman crying with her faced covered, mirroring Mary Magdalene on the opposite side as they are the only two not looking at Jesus or the Virgin Mary. Mary Salome is the woman in the green dress holding the Virgin Mary. The Virgin Mary has fainted and her skin is so pale that it has become deathlike, imitating her son, who is dead (although he has a healthier skin colour). Then comes the bearded gentleman with the red skullcap who is Nicodemus, who along with the unidentified person on the ladder and the man holding the jar in the background (who has been identified as a servant to Joseph of Arimathea) are the only people not crying. This may be because although present and involved with the crucifixion and deposition, Nicodemus was not one of Jesus's followers (assumedly the man on the cross and the servant weren't either). John the Evangelist is in red and the wealthy clad gentleman in gold is Joseph of Arimathea (the person who donated his tomb to bury Jesus), both of them are crying. The jar of ointment is for the corpse.

Finally, have a look at the cross again, it is clearly too small to have supported anyone's weight. However, Van der Weyden does not have any issues about reducing the size of the cross to fit it into the picture and the composition in general.

### Why have I included this painting in this guidebook?

Because no matter what your faith, the *The Descent from the Cross* offers the viewer with a universal image of bereavement and grief that transcends the crucifixion story of Jesus.

### Mary Magdalene in her underclothes

A detail that is usually overlooked is the little pin that you can see on the red sleeve of Mary Magdalene's dress. This little pin helped attach the sleeve to the dress and the whole outfit would have been concealed by another outer dress, which she is not wearing but that the other women are wearing. Indeed, Mary Magdalene is depicted not quite fully dressed and this would have been obvious to the viewers in the 15th century. Even Mary Magdalene's hair headdress is not quite in place. All this suggests that she was not quite prepared to leave the privacy of her home when she was summoned to the crucifixion, and that she left in haste. The fact that Mary Magdalene, former Biblical prostitute, is not quite dressed seems ichonographically appropriate.

## Guild of Crossbowmen of Leuven

Although it sounds like the title of a fairy-tale, these were the people who paid for the painting that would hang in their local church. As was customary, patrons usually received some sort of recognition in the paintings they commissioned. In the case of this picture there are not only two little cross bows painted into the false frame but also, Jesus and the Virgin Mary have both adopted *crossbow* postures with their bent outstretched arms.

## Van der Weyden

Little is known of Van der Weyden's life. Born in the 15th century, he is considered one of the most important Pre-Renaissance Flemish painters. During his lifetime he enjoyed a successful career in his hometown of Tournai and later in Brussels, receiving as well regular international commissions for his work. Likewise, he was probably considered the most popular and successful Flemish artist of his time and definitely the most influential.

Surprisingly, only three surviving paintings are considered securely authenticated works by Rogier van der Weyden, one of them is *The Descent from the Cross* you have in front of you.

## 13. The Last Supper by Juan de Juanes

Bottom floor - Room 52 C – Route B

**What's the picture about?**

Following classic Christian iconographic representations of the Last Supper, Jesus is represented at a table with his 12 apostles. Jesus and his followers have organised dinner to celebrate the Jewish Passover and have feasted accordingly. However, in the picture, Jesus has just announced that the party is over and has told his followers that he will be detained and executed. The apostles react in different guises of shock (even Judas), while Jesus impervious continues his speech about the bread becoming his body. Therefore, the exact moment depicted is the consecration of the bread and hence the institution of the Eucharist rite. For those not familiar with Christian rites, the celebration of the Eucharist is the core ritual identifying Christians and their belief. This would explain why Jesus is looking straight at us, as he is not only explaining the Eucharist to his apostles but is also apparently proselytising us, the viewers.

The follow up to this chapter of the Easter events can be found in the *Christ Crucified* by Velázquez and *The Descent from the Cross* by Van der Weyden, in this guide.

## Elements in the painting

*The Last Supper* is one of those fun paintings that have just enough interpretable elements to make it interesting, but not too many that it becomes overwhelming.

### The guests

To start with, the painting clearly evokes Leonardo da Vinci's Last Supper as everyone seems to be crowded around the table but leaving the front (and the figure of Christ) clear, as if on a stage. However, it is unlikely that de Juanes ever left Spain and his crowded disposition of the apostles and Jesus around one side of the table was fairly common at the time.

Apart from Jesus who is sitting in the middle and raising the Eucharist, the other figure that stands out is Judas who we can identify because he does not have a halo over his head and his name is engraved on his chair rather than floating within a halo as the rest of his colleagues. However there is more; to highlight his perfidious nature, de Juanes has depicted Judas as a red hair (nothing in the Gospels about this), which was associated (in medieval Europe) with moral degeneration and untrustworthiness. And if that was not enough, de Juanes has also clothed him in yellow, which is the colour of traitors, and pointed both knives at the table towards him. The final incriminating evidence is the purse he is holding in his right hand, which would contain the 30 silver coins he was paid for his treachery.

### The table

On the table remain some bread, salt, and half an orange along with a carafe of red wine, a chalice, a platter and two knives. Presumably the mandatory Passover lamb dinner has been cleared away.

Note how the Eucharist that Jesus is holding resembles our current day Eucharist made from unleavened bread (no yeast), however, the rest of the bread on the table clearly contains yeast. Although artists started to use leavened bread in their depictions of the Last Supper so as to facilitate understanding of what was going on, Jesus and his followers would never have, as this is one of the main proscriptions to celebrate the Jewish Passover Dinner (there wouldn't have been yeast in the whole house). So the question remains, where did Jesus find that Eucharist if only loaves of bread are available on the table?

The red wine we see will be promptly consecrated becoming the blood of Christ. Jesus will use the chalice that is in front of him which is a copy of the chalice guarded in the Cathedral of Valencia in Spain and said to be the authentic Holy Grail used at the Last Supper. This painting was commissioned by the Cathedral of Valencia, so it makes sense that they would have asked de Juanes to authenticate their relic in painting.

There is also a saltcellar depicted on the table, which is a commonly used religious symbol associated with Christ as well as being one of the most valued commodities (salt) until fairly recent times. Unsurprisingly, Judas is believed to have spilt the salt at the Last Supper, so not only was he wasting a very expensive item but also symbolically rejecting Christ; thus the Western superstition of spilling salt at a table as being bad luck.

The half orange may serve as a reminder that the main course of the Last Supper had been fish and not lamb. In the 16th century the use of citric fruits with fish had become a rage (and things have not changed too much 400 years later as fish is still commonly served with a slice of lemon). This change in the Last Supper menu may appear trivial, however, for the Church it would have been essential as they transformed the most important Jewish festivity into the most important Christian one. And substituting the Jewish Passover lamb for the Christian fish (fish may have been the first Christian symbol) makes sense.

*Other elements*

In front of the table are depicted a pitcher and a basin. These were used prior to the dinner to wash the feet of those present (note how they are all barefoot). Apparently it was customary (and expected from the host to provide water) to wash your feet on entering a home in Jesus's time, especially as you would have been running around all day in sandals. In the Gospels it is Jesus who shocks his disciples and washes their feet, which would have been inappropriate as it would have been a servant performing these duties.

Finally, I have always found it odd that most Last Supper depictions take place during the daytime. However, the Gospels clearly state that the Last Supper was a meal served in the evening.

## Why have I included this painting in this guidebook?

No matter what the experts say, I believe that this Last Supper is much more pleasing to the eye than Leonardo's hyped up one and lots of fun to interpret.

## Juan de Juanes

Not much is known of the life of Juan de Juanes and his life appears to have been fairly uneventful. He was the son and apprentice of the renowned Spanish painter Vicent Maçip, born at the beginning of the 16th century and is one of the best-known examples of Renaissance artists in Spain. Following the footsteps of his father, he made a successful reputation for himself in his home region of Valencia as a religious painter.

It appears that he also received a classic intellectual education and was well cultivated in humanist and literary circles of his time. Unsurprisingly, Valencia was one of the main ports through which Italian Renaissance ideals entered Spain. This admiration for Latin antiquity may have led him to change his name from Maçip to the more Latin name de Juanes (I doubt his father was to happy with this).

## Super-size my Last Supper

A recent academic study that analysed 52 Last Supper scenes in western art comparing head size ratios to food serving sizes found that over the last 1000 years the entrees grew by 70% and the bread by 23%. This confirmed the study's hypothesis that food portions had increased over time and that different moments in time have normalised their food intake (or at least the intake of those that could afford to eat well). The *Last Supper* by de Juanes made the cut and now that they mention it, the loaves of bread indeed appear to be bread roll size.

## 14. The Third of May 1808 by Goya

Bottom floor - Room 65 – Route B

### What's the picture about?

The first thing that comes to mind when facing the picture is that we are not looking at a *typical* historical painting. The picture looks more like a *Pulitzer Prize* photograph than the commemoration of a historical event. Or in other words, the painting resembles more a *snapshot* of the event, where no one is posing and nothing has been theatrically prepared; what Goya saw or imagined (there is no evidence that he actually was there at the execution place) is what he painted.

The next issue is the theme; Goya is commemorating the event as historical paintings do, but he is commemorating the anonymous people of Madrid. There is no protagonist, no general or king that is being honoured in this painting, only the execution of everyday people. This is also unprecedented in historical paintings.

Finally, Goya is also condemning the brutality of war. He is obviously not the first to paint violence and death in a historical painting. However, he may have been the first to paint it without glorifying it. The people are dead or going to die and the spectator unwillingly empathises with the victims. This had not happened before in art where soldiers were either heroically dead or dying in battle. There is no heroism or bling in the *Third of May 1808*, only desperation and meaningless brutality; Goya has rubbed away the shine from war and exposed its cruel reality. In fact, it would be hard to tell that the firing squad is French if it were not for the title. Goya does not appear to be too interested in clearly identifying the *evil* French invader and oppressor. Rather, the firing squad appears to represent *all* meaningless violence that *all* wars represent while the executed may represent all the suffering of *all* war victims. All of this this was something unheard of in historical painting until (and even after) Goya.

**Elements in the painting**

The painting depicts the execution by firing squad of what appears to be group of men who are clearly not soldiers (there even appears to be a monk amongst them). On the ground are strewn the bodies of the dead while in the background another group await their fate. This event took place on the 3rd of May of 1808 and it corresponds to the aftermath of the insurrection that took place on the 2nd of May of 1808 (hence the titles of the two paintings you are looking at).

**Why have I included this painting in this guidebook?**

The *Third of May 1808* has not made the cut for this guidebook because of the historic importance of the events it describes, but rather, because of the genius with which Goya represented the events using an expressionist *language* and technique almost 100 years ahead of his time. Indeed, we would have to wait to the early 20th century and specifically to the German avant-garde expressionist movement to find a painting that recalls this one. Goya would later take this expressionist technique to the extreme with his *Black Paintings*.

Regarding the pseudo-expressionist technique employed in *The Third of May*, Goya literally avoids precision and realism. Take a look at the execution squad and how close they are standing to the victims. Goya is more interested in the overall dramatic effect obtained by the repetition of soldiers that make up the firing squad (especially their muskets) who are standing at an impossibly near range to the victims. This thechnique also allows Goya to zoom in on the victims and through very broad and bold brush strokes, dramatise the light effects (where on earth did they find that floodlight in 19th century Spain?), express little concern for anatomical proportions or perspective correction, and almost no interest for detail (the white shirt is a shirt, does it matter what its made of?). The painting almost has the feel of a low quality and slightly blurred photograph and yet all this pictorial *unrealism* dotes the painting with deeper meaning than if Goya had simply painted a classic academic representation of the event.

And as I mentioned previously, it would take artists almost a hundred year more to venture again into the realms of *expression* over *representation*.

## The French invasion and Spanish Independence War

The story behind the picture requires a short crash course in early 19th century Spanish history, and to understand these tragic events and understand what is going on (who are these people?, and who are the soldiers?) we have to rewind a year to 1807, when Spain unwisely decided to take sides with Napoleon (then emperor of France) and help invade Portugal.

The inept and cuckolded Spanish king Charles IV was deceived by his then Prime Minister, Gody, and his (in theory the King's but there are rumours that it may have been Godoy's as he was apparently sleeping with the queen) son, the future Ferdinand VII into allowing French troops into Spain on their way to Portugal. Godoy (and the future Ferdinand VII) had likewise negotiated behind Charles IV's back that when the time came to divide Portugal, he would keep the southern part as his own feud, whilst France would keep the lion's share and Spain would get a small section in the north. What no one expected was that Napoleon intended to double-cross them all and place his brother on the throne of Spain.

In this manner, and after a year of apathy in which several major cities in Spain were already effectively under French rule, Charles IV decided to abdicate in favour of his son (Ferdinand VII) whilst

Godoy was ousted from Government (Charles IV was already on route out of Spain having realised that he had lost all power). However, Ferdinand VII was quickly disposed of and forced into exile to France in favour of Napoleon's brother, the future Joseph I. By then (assuming you have been able to follow all these intrigues), the people had had enough and rebelled against the French, thus starting the Independence War against the French.

The official date for the start of the war is the 2nd of May, when the good people of Madrid (citizens, not army) rioted and managed to kill over a 100 French soldiers. The French garrison in control of the city quickly subdued the insurrection and retaliated. Prisoners taken were executed on the 3rd of May. That is what you are looking at, the execution of the people of Madrid by French soldiers and the beginning of the brutal Independence War. The war ended in 1814 with the defeat of the French and the crowning of Ferdinand VII as king.

One final note, you may have noticed that several of the horsemen in the other painting (*Second of May 1808*) appear to be Arab in appearance; and they were, part of the French army was made up of Arab mercenaries.

## Goya and the War

The French invasion in 1807 and later Spanish Independence War (1808-1814) became an essential motif in Goya's artistic production. Not only through several of his paintings but perhaps more importantly through his prints (mainly the series titled *Disasters of the War*, some of which are displayed in the Prado). Indeed, perhaps his most notable paintings, the *Black Paintings* frescoes, are thought to have developed from a pessimistic or nihilist view of the world and human nature in general (these were all painted after the war and towards the end of his life). However, in the case of the *Third of May 1808* and its sister painting the *Second of May 1808*, Goya adopts a much more condemning (and also commemorative) perspective. Goya's *Disasters of the War* (the prints), produced at around the same time as the *third of May 1808*, are possibly much more critical and condemning of the random and unjustified violence that characterise war on all sides.

## 15. Vulcan's Forge by Velázquez

Top floor - Room 11 – Route B

### What's the picture about?

Apollo is at Vulcan's forge, which suspiciously looks like a Spanish (or Italian) forge from the 17th century, and is telling Vulcan about his wife. The news must be a bit disturbing as Vulcan and his team, have stopped working and are intently listening. Apollo is not being very discreet, as he has decided to publicly share some very embarrassing news.

Apart from a pretext to execute several extraordinary male anatomical studies in a realist and naturalist setting following Baroque guidelines (this painting was done during what can be considered Velázquez's formative years), art historians generally agree that *Vulcan's Forge* contains an allegory that Velázquez would return to recurrently over his life: the claim that Art is a spiritual and noble profession in opposition to craftsmanship, which was considered base and manual.

Thus, Apollo, the god of the sun and also of the arts, would represent the spiritual, aristocratic and intellectual capacity of the fine arts, such as painting, in opposition to Vulcan, his team and his forge who would represent manual labour intrinsic to all crafts.

This may not seem to important for us now but at the time, in the rigid class systems that prevailed in Europe, how you made your living would drastically condition your possibilities of social success and fortune. In summary, higher classes did not work with their hands but with their heads, and if you wanted to belong to their club, you couldn't work with your hands either (kind of hard for a painter).

The painting must have also been important for Velázquez, as it was not painted for a commission and Velázquez kept if in his own private collection until it was eventually sold to Philip IV years later.

**Elements in the painting**

The setting is a blacksmith's forge. Velázquez has depicted the forge in classic naturalist baroque style and what we are looking at is probably very close to what Velázquez saw at his local blacksmith's back in the day. That said, I doubt the blacksmiths were as elegant and attractive as the ones depicted in this painting. So Velázquez probably integrated models that conformed to classic canons into a forge setting.

Like all Baroque paintings, *Vulcan's Forge* is full of anachronisms. Anachronisms (something belonging to another time period, such as Roman soldiers in medieval knight armour) were commonplace in European art, especially when it came to mythological or biblical paintings. In most cases, this was due to a lack of imagination or documentation by the well-intentioned painters. However, in the case of this painting, Velázquez intentionally highlights the anachronism of the subjects.

Therefore, what is left of the mythological story at Vulcan's forge is an *everyday scene* at any of the local 17th century forges, to the extent that the figure that appears out of place is Apollo (the gentleman with a halo and wearing a tunic) as the rest of the scene would have been contemporary to Velázquez.

## Why have I included this painting in this guidebook?

Because everybody likes a good cuckold story.

## Vulcan's forge as told by Ovid in his Metamorphosis

The story, as told by Ovid in his Metamorphosis, goes as follows. Apollo, god of the sun, has come to tell Vulcan, god of fire, volcanoes and smiths, that his wife Venus, goddess of love and beauty, is cheating on him with Mars, god of war. Apollo is not particularly a friend of Vulcan's, none of the gods were, and I sincerely believe that this whole event is in rather bad taste. However, Vulcan decides to retaliate, as many upset husbands tend to do, and forges a net strong enough to trap Mars and his wife. He then discovers their love niche while they are busy doing whatever lovers do, and casting the net over them traps them *in delicto*. Vulcan calls the rest of the gods who have a jolly good time ridiculing the two best-looking of the gods. The story ends with a shamed Venus returning to the forge and behaving herself (for a while at least).

The story is better appreciated if you consider that Venus was betrothed by her father Jupiter (King of the gods) to Vulcan so as to avoid possible conflicts amongst the other male gods (you make sure your relatives don't kill each other over a woman by giving her to the ugliest male). Apparently Venus was not too happy about this (surprise). Vulcan was not only an old man, but walked with a limp and was hunchbacked. Velázquez left out the hunchback but provided Vulcan with a beard (he is the gentleman facing you, with the goatee staring at Apollo). Velázquez also decided to convert Vulcan's team in the forge, the Cyclopes (one eyed humanoid monsters), into human beings.

The final twist in the story comes when you realise that Vulcan's team is busy preparing some armour; I assume you can guess whom it is for (hint: what god is always at war?).

## Golden ratio and *rabatment* of the rectangle

Velázquez was a master of composition. This does not mean that he was born with an innate ability to do this but rather, that he received solid theoretical training in this field during his years of apprenticeship.

What is meant by a painting being well composed and balanced is that the picture is unconsciously pleasing to the viewer. Therefore, and regardless of your prior knowledge, your brain will tell you whether a picture is balanced or not. Indeed, artists have also deliberately used these techniques to obtain the opposite effect on the viewer by creating *disturbing* images, simply by unbalancing the elements in the composition.

In the case of *Vulcan's Forge*, Velázquez has used a classic *rabatment* of the rectangle technique, which is based on the golden ratio. And because he has used this compositional technique, you, or rather, your brain (as you are probably not even aware of it) finds the painting pleasing and balanced.

*Rabatment of the rectangle*

Paintings tend to be rectangle shaped for a reason. A rectangle allows the artist to compose a picture starting with a square shaped area and then adding a space to this square shaped area creating the overall rectangle. Our brain (whether we want to or not) focuses first on the square shaped area and then on the overall rectangle shape of the picture.

If the space that is added to the square shaped area follows certain proportions (golden section proportions), then the overall composition is balanced and therefore, pleasant to the viewer. I must reiterate that all of this happens without the viewer being aware of anything; humans are simply wired to *read* pictures this way.

Furthermore, the square shaped area will usually contain the bulk of the information in the picture, thus reinforcing the natural path of our gaze when looking at the painting.

*Golden ratio*

For the record, the golden ratio can be defined as follows: *"two quantities are in the golden ratio if their ratio is the same as the ratio of their sum to the larger of the two quantities."* This enigmatic and almost incomprehensible formulation is found in *Vulcan's Forge*.

## 16. Crucifixion by Velázquez

Top floor - Room 14 – Route B

**What's the picture about?**

The picture depicts the most important iconographic image for the Church: the image of Jesus Christ, the Son of the Christian God, at the moment of his crucifixion, and in this case, after having died, although his body continues erect. The representation of a crucified Christ served the obvious purpose of proselytisation, or in other words, it is a pictorial advertisement of the main event in Christian belief.

This is one of the few religious paintings attributed to Velázquez, as he was usually busy painting for the king. Remember that back in the day it was either the royalty/nobility or the Church that commissioned paintings.

## Elements in the painting

Christ is depicted on the cross crucified. None of the other actors in the story are represented and the background is a plain sombre grey. The inscription above Jesus's head is in three languages: Hebrew, Greek and Latin. In the tradition of 17th century art, Christ has had a full body wax.

Velázquez presents a classic crucified Christ modelled after Apollo (the mythological Greek god that was commonly depicted as the ideal male). The classic posture is reinforced by the use of four nails instead of the commonly used three nails (one for each hand and one through both feet). The use of four nails allows for Christ to adopt the classic stance with a raised right hip and the weight of his body on his left leg. Indeed, if it were not for the cross and the raised arms, we could be looking at any classic Greek or Roman sculpture. The almost lack of blood and the serenity in Christ's semblance also reinforce this idea. It is as if the painting were more a study of male anatomy than a representation of Christ crucified. The body has conveniently been illuminated from an unidentified light source facing Jesus, more or less from where you are standing.

Jesus is also depicted with his characteristic crown of thorns and a halo around his head emphasising his divine nature. The wound in his side is the alleged *coup de grace* provided by the spear of the Roman soldier Longinus who in an act of humanity put Christ out of his agony.

An unverified theory regarding this painting is that Jesus's face is unconventionally covered by his hair because Velázquez got tired of painting his facial factions and decided to hurry up the job by covering half the face with hair.

## Why have I included this painting in this guidebook?

Because everyone likes a naughty story, and this painting has a great one.

Also, this depiction of Christ on the cross may be one of the most captivating male anatomical studies in art history.

## Naughty Philip IV

Apparently, Phillip IV (the king) took a fancy for one of the young novices at the local convent of San Placido in Madrid, which still stands. How he came to see and meet her is not explained. In any case, a passionate affair began, perhaps more on the king's side than hers, to the extent that a secret entrance was made into the convent from a neighbouring building so that the king could access the convent at his leisure. Conveniently, no one in the convent head anything and nothing was discovered until it was too late. To hush up the scandal, apart from the usual economic compensations, this painting was also commissioned and presented to the convent. The painting hung in the sacristy until it was taken in the 19th century by the Spanish Prime Minister Godoy (more on him in *The Third of May 1808* and *The Nude Maja*, both by Goya) and ultimately it ended up in the Prado as part of the royal collection.

There is another version to the story where the painting was commissioned for the same sins, but these were committed by a Mr. Villanueva, a royal secretary, and not by the king. Mr. Villanueva was apparently processed by the Inquisition for events associated with this convent, but it is unclear if whether he was tried accused of naughtiness or as an accomplice. In any case, as no one knows who this chap is, the one with the king is much more entertaining. And finally, there is always the possibility that the Court just felt really generous with this convent and decided to commission and donate the painting. I find this last option hard to believe as it would require using the official court painters time as well as have cost money.

## Crosses and crucifixions

The central part of the story of Jesus is his crucifixion and it is this image that has undoubtedly been represented most times in the Christian artistic repertoire. The classic Latin cross has currently become the most widely used cross when depicting Jesus's crucifixion. However, previous to this Latin the cross, earlier representations of Jesus crucified used the cross in the shape of a *T*. Artists in Northern Europe would continue to use the *T* cross even after the Latin cross became popular in other parts of Europe (See the chapter *The Descent from the Cross* by Van der Weyden for an example of a *T* shaped cross).

Interestingly (and I am aware that this may be very controversial for some readers), the use of a cross to depict the crucifixion (and by default the symbol of Christian faith) is a historic convention that was apparently assumed at least a century after the founding of the Church. The Gospels do not specifically state that a cross was used but rather that Jesus was executed on a *stauros* (this is a Greek word used in the Gospels and basically meaning stake as in upright pole). However, it is also possible that Jesus would have carried (as other criminals did in Roman times), his own crossbar to which he would have been fastened and then hoisted to the stake, which was already buried in the ground.

## 17. Nude Maja by Goya

Top floor - Room 36 – Route B

**What's the picture about?**

Perhaps Goya's *Nude Maja* represents the culmination of centuries of disguised images of objectified female sexuality. Female nudes have been a constant in western art since the Middle Ages and it appears that nobility and royalty have always felt the need to commission female nudes under the guise of allegorical and exemplifying mythological themes (eg. Titian's *Venuses*, Botticelli's *Birth of Venus*, Velazquez's *Rokeby Venus*...); and clearly Venus was always a favourite (goddess of love and beauty). Unsurprsingly, the commissioners of these allegorical paintings have always been males.

Therefore, I believe I would not be too far off the mark if I assumed that chauvinist male urges regarding the consumption of titillating imagery has always existed (what we now refer to as erotic or pornographic pictures). Indeed, it would not be until Manet, more than 60 years later, that this statement was finally made with his *Olympia*, forcing both connoisseurs and spectators to publically admit what they were truly admiring, that is, the body of a nude female who has been represented so as to exhibit her female sexual attributes. Predictably, one of the first and most widespread uses found for photography (and cinema) from the very beginning was the production and marketing of erotic and pornographic images.

## Elements in the painting

A nude woman lying on her back on a couch (or bed) and looking directly at the viewer.

## Why have I included this painting in this guidebook?

Because I find intriguing how the *Nude Maja* has become one of Goya's best known and appreciated paintings. Moreover if you consider that: a) the picture itself is (arguably) poorly painted, b) was never hung in a public place, and c) has no allegorical pretentions. I will now consider these claims below, starting with the last one.

## My claims:

There is clearly no allegorical intention. The painting represents a nude woman displaying herself and on a bed, and she is not Venus. We know she is not Venus as the painting has never been inventoried as such but rather as the *Nude Maja*. A *Maja* in Spanish simply means young pretty woman. And the truth is we do not know who this woman is. There are claims suggesting that the *Maja* is the Duchess of Alba, a lover of Goya, which I find absurd as they are based more on the need to justify a painting of this nature than any tangible fact; as if this painting were a trophy of true love rather than lust. It is hard for art historians and museums to accept that this painting may simply be an idealised image of a nude woman; and that the only intention is to tantalise its viewers.

The painting, until displayed in the Prado, was never hung in a public place. This was a painting commissioned by an individual and hung in a private home for his own enjoyment. The individual was Godoy and the private location was his private getaway in Madrid. Mr Godoy was the Prime Minister at the Spanish Royal Court and therefore he could do this, that is, commission paintings from an official court painter. It also appears that he was a bit of a naughty gentleman as he commissioned this painting for his own use and fun. Hanging next to the *Nude Maja* is the *Clothed Maja*, what appears to be an exact replica of the nude one, but this time clothed hiding all her sexual attributes. These paintings were painted at the same time and hung together, however, thanks to a cleverly devised mechanism, depending on who was present in the room, only one of the two was displayed (the other disappeared behind the displayed painting into the wall). So, it is not hard to imagine our naughty Mr. Godoy having a good ol' time with his mates and the *Nude Maja* and then, if there was an unexpected visit, hitting a *panic button* (most likely some sort of lever), thus hiding the naughty *Maja* and displaying the correct but less enticing *Dressed Maja*. Although this may be hard to believe, there is evidence that this is all true. In this manner and putting it bluntly, Goya's *Nude Maja* is really only a 19th century Playboy centre-fold.

Finally, although Goya is considered one of the greatest masters of all time, the *Nude Maja* is poorly painted. She is reclining on a bed but there is no way any body would recline how she is able to (give it a try). However, to fully exhibit her sexual attributes, Goya decided to ignore gravity and her anatomy, thus she is completely facing us, suspended in the air. Gravity is thrown out of the window again when painting her breasts. It is impossible for her breasts to rest in the manner that they are resting, or in other words, her right breast would fall towards her left one. However, if the intention is to exalt her breasts, this obviously works better with them separated. Finally, her neck, or rather the lack of, is all wrong. Her head has been almost stuck on as if someone had done a bad cut-and-paste with Photoshop. Once again, what is important for Goya was to represent the sexuality in her face (full lips, blushed cheeks, dilated pupils, bold gaze... these are classic and still used sexually charged facial attributes in depicting women). What Goya does is objectify a female body to the extent that we read the picture as a sum of parts (although these parts do not case well together) and still find the picture pleasing. When I say we, I refer to both men and women, as women have (unfortunately) been trained to *look and see* by our male dominated and chauvinist society.

**Reasons to exhibit this painting in a museum**

Regarding the question of how the *Nude Maja* has become one of Goya's most well known and celebrated paintings, the answer is unclear. Perhaps art historians could not accept that one of our (Spanish) masters would have painted this, and decided that by hanging the painting in one of the greatest museums in the world alongside other masterpieces, the painting automatically becomes higher art that transcends the mundane. Or perhaps they were just pleasantly tickled by the image and decided to share it with all of us, in which case, they have my eternal gratitude.

## 18. Sisyphus by Titian

Top floor – Stairs – Route B

### What's the picture about?

Sisyphus was a mythological Greek King who not only boasted divine ascendants (possibly Poseidon) but also descendants of epic proportions (Bellerophontes, who killed the Chimera). However, Sisyphus is better known for being your everyday arrogant, violent, avaricious and deceitful Greek ruler. Amongst other qualities he would randomly kill travellers and even guests, attempted fratricide, got his sister-in-law pregnant (possibly raped) and mocked the gods. Clearly with all of this in his résumé he was bound to end badly.

The last straw was when he tricked Death himself and upset the Underworld. Sisyphus was condemned in Hell to the pointless activity of rolling a boulder up a steep hill for eternity. The twist in the punishment is that just when Sisyphus is about to reach the top of the hill the boulder always slips away and rolls down the hill again. In this manner Sisyphus has been associated with any pointless and/or apparently impossible activities.

Sisyphus belonged to a series of four paintings commissioned by Mary of Austria (a renown art collector in her time and sister to the Emperor Charles V) for her palace in the Netherlands. The unifying theme was the condemnation and punishment of four mythological Greek characters who dared defy the gods. Of the four, only two have survived and both are in the Prado. If you look around you may see a painting (similar in size to this one) representing a man chained down having his liver eaten by an eagle; that's Tityos being punished. The other two that were lost in a fire were Ixion and Tantalus.

However, what you may find more surprising is the unifying theme of the four paintings. Each one describes the punishment of these classic mythological characters. And their punishments are pretty brutal. Why Mary of Austria chose this theme is unclear. She may have been interested in presenting an allegory of the difficulties of governance to her subjects, or perhaps she was attempting to send a subtle warning to the separatist Dutch separatist leaders. Or perhaps she just had a morbid fascination for torture and pain.

There is evidence that she was not happy with her post as governor of the Netherlands during the time these paintings were commissioned (remember that current day Netherlands and Belgium were part of the Spanish Empire during the 16th and 17th century and were continuously upset with political, nationalist and religious turmoil).

## Elements in the painting

Sisphyus is represented as a muscular male (recalling somewhat Michaelangelo's nudes), carrying a large boulder up a hill. He is in Hell as it is dark and there is fire and lava in the background; there also appears to be two monstrous creatures watching his progress. Titian has decided to alter the story somewhat and Sisyphus is carrying the boulder up the hill and not rolling it up; this allows to enhance the overall dramatic effect of the image as Sisyphus is also weighed down by the boulder as he struggles up the slope.

## Why have I included this painting in this guidebook?

The myth of Sisyphus offers a wide range of interpretations and artists, philosophers and writers throughout history have frequently resorted to it. Perhaps it's the simplicity of the punishment and the absence of unnecessary violence and gore that have made it one of the more popular punishment myths (it is hard to propose an existentialist allegory when the subject requires a man getting his liver pecked out as in the case of Tityos).

In this manner, few images are neither more powerful nor iconographic in classic Greek mythological imaginary than Sisyphus and his boulder. Titian understood all of this perfectly as he has presented us with a colossal, and yet human, Sisyphus with whom we inadvertently empathise as the figure obviates his evil doings and recalls the strain of forced physical labour.

## Defiance and punishment in Greek mythology

The complete series commissioned by Mary of Austria was made up of the following Greek myths:

**Sisyphus** was made to push or carry a boulder up a hill for eternity. However, just as he was about to reach the top and complete his task, the boulder would fall away and roll back down the hill.

His crime: continuous deceit and arrogance that ended up annoying the gods. He is credited for having escaped from Hell by tricking Thanatos (Death) into freeing him and then trapping Thanatos. This caused a major uproar on earth, as without Thanatos, humans could no longer die.

**Tityos** was a giant sent to Hell where he was chained and endured two vultures that would peck out and eat his liver every day for all eternity. His liver would grow back every night.

His crime: attempted rape of Leto, the mother of Apollo and Artemis. The twist in the story is that Tityos was following orders by Hera, who in turn was retaliating against her husband's (Zeus) liaison with Leto.

**Tantalus** was trapped in a pool of water up to his knees, with a fruit tree just above him. However, he could not reach the fruit on the tree to satiate his hunger nor drink the water, which would recede, to quench his thirst; all of this for eternity.

His crime: sharing the gods' secrets with mortals, stealing their ambrosia and nectar and killing and eating his son at a feast for the gods. That's infanticide, cannibalism, theft and treason.

**Ixion** was tied with snakes to a fiery wheel in Hell and condemned to spin around for eternity.

His crime: he murdered his father-in-law by casting him into a pit of hot coals and then attempted to bed Hera, Zeus's wife. He did manage to couple with Zeus, who presented himself to Ixion transformed into Hera. You have to love these gods.

## Titian and the Spanish Court

The Italian painter Titian was an all time favourite with the Spanish Habsburg dynasty. Titian would not only paint regularly for Charles V but also for his sister (Mary of Austria) and his son, the future Philip II. In the case of Philip II, the patronage would begin before he was crowned king. Surprisingly, however, there is no account of Titian ever visiting Spain. The few times he met the Spanish royalty was in Germany.

However, Titian can be considered a Spanish Court painter as he received regular commissions from Philip II during most of his life, including his famed erotic series. Thanks to this relationship with the Spanish Court, the Prado now boasts one of the best collections of works by Titian in the whole world.

## 19. Democritus by Ribera

Top floor - Room 8 – Route B

## What's the picture about?

This is a portrait of Democritus, the famed Greek philosopher who was born 400 years before our Christian era. Or rather, this an imaginary portrait of Democritus as there are no surviving images of Democritus from his time nor could Ribera have guessed what he looked like. So if we ignore the title of the painting and look again, what we are probably looking at is the portrait of some anonymous deprived working-class man from the 17th century with a goofy smile.

This does not mean that the portrait is not supposed to be Democritus, the fact that he is holding a compass and that there are mathematical and geometry illustrations on the papers is reason enough to believe that we have the title correct. However, Ribera, who appears to have a sense of humour, has also decided to give Democritus a very silly smile. However, this does not answer our question of why Ribera painted a grinning Democritus disguised as a poor person.

To answer this question we need to firstly take into account that painting impoverished philosophers was a common genre in 17th century Baroque (Baroque is the art movement that followed the Renaissance) painting in Europe. Or in other words, it was in fashion to paint great Classic Greek and Roman intellectuals as *beggar philosophers*. Indeed, Ribera would later be commissioned a series of six imaginary *beggar philosophers* by the Prince of Liechtenstein. The reason behind this was that these paintings were meant to symbolically illustrate a philosopher's pursuit for knowledge and enlightenment to the extent that he renounces all material and mundane pleasures and comforts. European aristocracy in the 17th century loved this idea and painters obliged.

However, Ribera went a step further and decided to paint his *Democritus beggar philosopher* as a beggar posing as a philosopher. What Ribera has achieved with this painting is to dignify (even with the goofy smile) the destitute of his society through an ironic representation of aristocratic collective imaginary. It is if Ribera had visually said to his patrons and those that had access to his work: there is nothing dignified about being a beggar, poverty denigrates the mind and the body; and there is no way a beggar would waste his time resolving mathematical problems with a compass. And this is exactly what the grin on Democritus is telling us.

## Elements in the painting

Democritus is depicted facing the viewer from roughly the waist up. He is standing in front of a table with papers and books. In his right hand he is holding a compass. Ribera has included several anachronisms (contemporary objects from the painter's time that would not have existed at the time depicted in the painting) in the painting such as Democritus's 17th century clothing and the book, which would not have existed in 300 BC as the printing press was invented 1800 years later. The papers he is holding appropriately contain mathematical and geometry diagrams.

However, Ribera does not forget that he is in reality portraying a beggar, or at least someone from a low social class, and depicts him accordingly, with dirty fingernails, messy facial hair and an unbecoming receding hairline. Likewise, his clothes are almost in tatters and even Democritus's decorum is lost as he barely conceals his bare chest.

All of this is painted in a chiaroscuro technique (dramatic contrasts between illuminated and dark areas in the painting), which was in vogue at the time and which would characterise all of Ribera's artistic production.

Ribera has signed the painting on the spine of the book as Jusepe de Ribera *Spaniard*.

### Why have I included this painting in this guidebook?

Because everyone loves a silly looking philosopher. Think about it, your average philosopher is depicted as a very serious old man with a manly beard and stern look, usually lost in his abstract and ethereal reflections. Democritus looks like someone you'd go have a drink with.

### Ribera the painter and Ribera the *Mafiosi*

Born in 1591, Ribera was a Spanish painter that lived most of is life in Naples, which although Italian was part of the Kingdom of Spain back then. He is considered one of the great Spanish Baroque masters and undoubtedly the one who took Caravaggio's chiaroscuro style to its ultimate consequences. His style, apart from the *tenebrism* that is intrinsic to all chiaroscuro paintings, is naturalistic to the extent that he appears to revel in people's singularities and even defects. There is little room for idealism in his work.

Ribera is mostly known for the violent subject of his paintings, mainly the torture and martyrdom of saints and the punishment of classic mythological characters. His paintings tend to be exaggerated and his brutal depictions of torture and violence never fail to disturb or even repulse. Ribera clearly had some sort of morbid fascination for human cruelty and reality. These themes were also very much in vogue at the time amongst aristocratic and religious circles.

A lesser-known aspect of Ribera is that he was not a nice guy. He may have empathised with the poor and destitute but his life is characterised by a Mafiosi lifestyle. Having first left Spain and the fled from Rome and its creditors, he settled down in Naples where he became the leader of the *Cabal of Naples.* The *Cabal* was essentially a Mafioso organisation that decided who could work as a painter in Naples. Defying the *Cabal* usually meant harassment, intimidation, sabotage, violence and eventually even poisoning and death. Literally, for a period that spanned between 1610 and 1640, no one could work as an artist in Naples without Ribera's consent.

Just a generation older than Ribera, the Italian artist and unofficial creator of the chiaroscuro technique, Caravaggio was also known for his tumultuous lifestyle, having to flee several times justice and landing in prison at least once for murder. Just goes to show that, as a professor once told me at school, we should never judge a work of art by the artist that painted it.

## 20. Birth of John the Baptist by Gentileschi

Top floor - Room 7 – Route B

**What's the picture about?**

The scene presents us with the aftermath of Elizabeth's successful birth of the future John the Baptist. According to the Bible, Elizabeth was the Virgin Mary's cousin and wife to the priest Zacharias. Christian belief recounts how the angel Gabriel appeared to Zacharias and announced that his wife would beget a son as the Lord was compassionate and did not want him to die childless. The shocked Zacharias then explained to Gabriel that it was perhaps a bit late as neither he, nor his wife, were any longer in child bearing age. This annoyed Gabriel who scolded him and punished him speechless till the birth of John (lesson learnt: don't contradict angels).

However, on closer inspection the painting reveals a bit more. In line with Gentileschi's personal view of her world and under the pretext of a typical Biblical scene, she has painted homage to women and their inherent worth. The four women who are surrounding the baby are the protagonists of the painting, and these four women, or at least one of them, are midwives. Indeed, midwives may have been one of the few skills and professions that were (until the 17th century) exclusively female and where men's presence was barred. There were no men in the delivery rooms.

The women appear oblivious of any male constraints in the painting; they are independent and clearly skilled, as they have just helped produce a very healthy looking child. They are also monumental, self-reliant, and relaxed. There is nothing delicate or effeminate about them, they are presented as robust women that do not need to rely on male paternal guidance or assistance. This is underlined again with the newborn, which appears to be safe and happy amongst them. Furthermore, the only male presence in the scene (apart from the newborn) is Zacaharias, who is being ignored (and ignoring in turn).

In a nutshell, I believe this is a bold, albeit cryptic, feminist statement in a society that could get you burnt at the stake for expressing feminist statements.

## Elements in the painting

The first thing that calls our attention is the disposition of the actors in the scene. The newborn baby John conventionally occupies the centre of the picture as expected. However, both Zacharias and possibly Elizabeth have been relegated to the back and periphery of the painting. In other words, they are clearly secondary actors. Meanwhile, Zacharias is busy writing a letter and his wife and an unidentified figure can be seen behind him in the shadows. It is interesting how Gentileschi depicts a very detached father who is more concerned with writing then celebrating the birth of his only son. In this manner, the women who are framing the baby while they finish bathing him are clearly the main actresses.

As was usual in 17th century Italian painting, the Biblical scene is depicted with realistic anachronism, as the room, objects, clothing and architecture are all clearly from the 17th century.

## Why have I included this painting in this guidebook?

Because it was painted by a woman, and in the 17th century!

More astounding, Gentileschi not only overcame dramatic personal issues but also managed to elbow her way into the male dominated artistic circles of her time achieving recognition and fame throughout Europe. Furthermore, the surname Gentileschi is now associated with Artemisia and not with her father Orazio, who wasn't a bad painter either but was and still is eclipsed by his daughter.

Finally, in line with the rest of Gentileschi's work, the subject here also allows the artist to make a subtle critique of male and female roles and power relations during her time.

## Artemisia Gentileschi

Artemisia Gentileschi was born in 1593 in Rome and Like Anguissola (see *Portarait of Philip II* by Anguissola in this guide for more information on Anguissola), she was an exception to the prevalent norm of her day that only men could become recognised artists. Indeed, Gentileschi was most likely the best known female artist of her time (she became better known than her father who was also an artist) and holds the honour of being the first women to be accepted into the prestigious Academy of the Arts of Drawing in Florence.

However, rather then for her artistic skill and for being a leading artist of the baroque movement, Gentileschi is now possibly best known for a tragic episode in her life and her choice of violent biblical themes depicted with gory detail, frequently with male victims. Art historians would have us believe that this choice in retributive and violent themes was a consequence of Gentileschi's rape and the later trial of her rapist who had refused to marry her (during which she was tortured).

In any case, what I find much more intriguing about Gentileschi is how she achieved her in-depth knowledge of human anatomy (male and female). Remember that the majority of female painters at the time did not have access to nude male (or female) models and usually had to conform with becoming primarily portrait painters (such as Anguissola). This was not the case of Gentileschi.

Several of Gentileschi's works were later attributed to male artists coetaneous to her (mainly her father). This phenomenon frequently happened in our male dominated chauvinist European art history. It appears that art historians found it difficult to accept that a woman could achieve fame and social recognition through male dominated professions and therefore changed the authorship to a male artist, thus easing their (and most likely their peers') peace of mind.

## Exercise in contemporary female equality

A painting by Gentileschi's father Orazio is also displayed in the Prado. However, although less known and arguably not as talented as his daughter, Orazio has not been relegated to a side room but is displayed in the main hall of the museum (exit the room you are in now and go to the main hall, and you will find his monumental *Moises saved from the Nile*). It appears that some types of prejudice may still be prevalent in Europe; unsurprisingly, not once during five years of art and art history instruction at the School of Fine Arts in Madrid was I introduced to Gentileschi or any other renowned female artist prior to the 20th century.

## Midwives in the 17th century

Contrary to the widely accepted and chauvinist cliché that prostitution is the world's oldest profession; I believe there is reason to believe that it was obstetrics (before women were forced to sell their bodies they were probably assisting other women to give birth). In this manner, there is evidence that since prehistoric times women have developed and informally transmitted their obstetric knowledge and skill.

But midwives have had it very difficult at certain periods in European history, especially during the Middle Ages and up to the 18th century. Women who had become important independent community members (most everyone eventually needed a midwife), or who were just able to do things that escaped your average male's understanding were often singled out as witches or worse. And what could be more mysterious and frightening for men than childbirth, an entire part of life, which they did not understand nor over which could they exercise any control.

However, the monopoly of women in this field gradually changed at the end of the 16th century and early 17th century, when the men of science decided that the time had come to end female freedom in the delivery rooms. This was obviously not good news for pregnant women who would suffer the consequences till the 20th century.

114

41009751R00068

Made in the USA
Lexington, KY
27 April 2015